Jesus said,

'Let the children come to me! Don't try to stop them.

People who are like these little children belong to the kingdom of God.

I promise you that you cannot get into God's kingdom,

unless you accept it the way a child does.'

Then Jesus took the children in his arms

and blessed them by placing his hands on them.

MARK 10:14–16 CEV

THIS BOOK BELONGS TO
Lucy H.Y. Hicks
A GIFT FROM
Auntie Edna
DATE
Jan 22nd 2010

Rhona Davies • Illustrated by Maria Cristina Lo Cascio

THE BARNABAS CLASSIC

CHILDREN'S BIBLE

CONTENTS

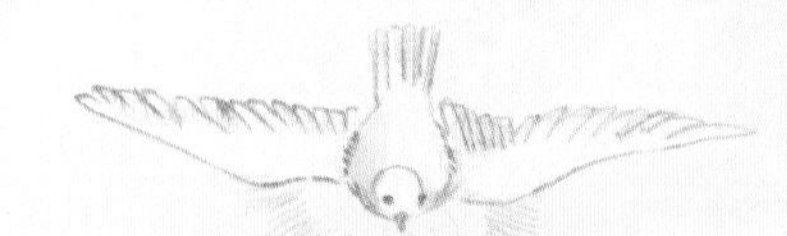

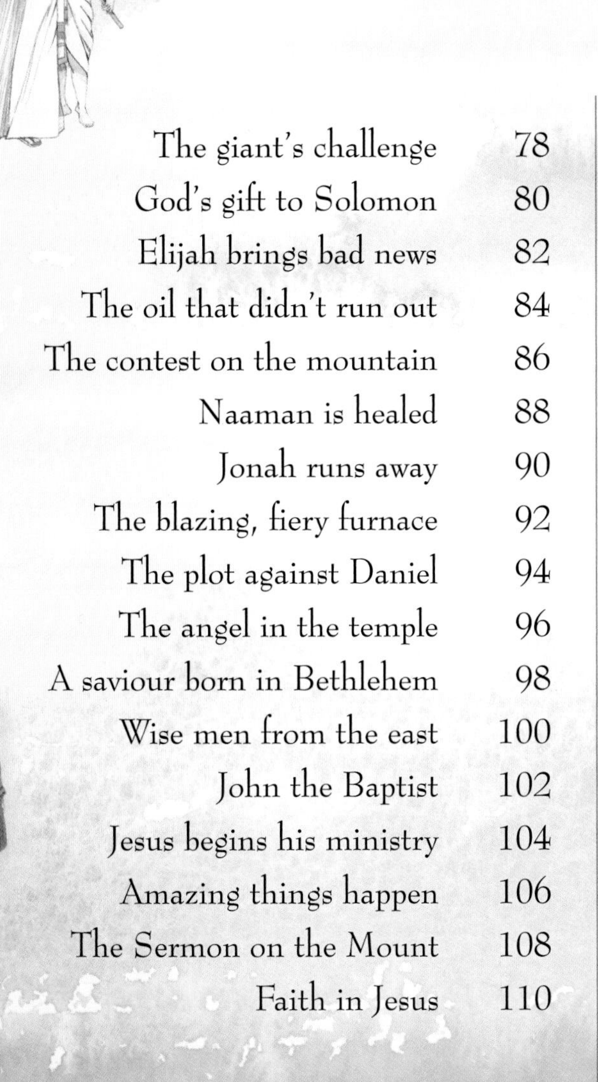

THE STORY OF CREATION

God looked at what he had done. All of it was very good!

GENESIS 1:31

In the beginning, long before the creation of the world, God was there.

'Let there be light!' God said. Light came into existence and God saw that the light was good. God divided the light, so that there was day and there was night.

Then God made the sky and separated it from the waters below. God brought the waters together into seas and created dry land.

'Let the land produce plants and trees full of seeds and fruits,' God said. Then the land was filled with every kind of green and leafy plant, from redwoods and chestnuts to cherry trees and strawberry plants. God saw that all he had made was good.

'Let there be lights in the sky for the night and the day,' God said. So the golden sun became the bright

light that shone in the day and the silvery moon the soft light that shone in the night sky. God scattered stars across the darkness of space and saw that all he had made was good.

'Let the waters and the skies be filled with every kind of creature that swims and flies. Let them multiply and increase in number.' Then there were dolphins and rainbow fish, kingfishers and peacocks, honey bees and beautiful butterflies. God saw that all he had made was good.

'Let there be all sorts of creatures to live on the land,' God said. So there were creatures that crawled and creatures that galloped. There were lumbering elephants and gentle giraffes, stripey tigers and chattering monkeys. God looked at everything he had made and saw that it was good.

Then God made man and woman and put them in charge of his creation. God looked at the beautiful world he had created and saw that it was very good, and then he rested.

Good and Evil

'You were made out of soil, and you will once again turn into soil.'

GENESIS 3:19

God loved the people he had made. He gave Adam and Eve a beautiful garden to live in, and he walked and talked with them every day. Adam and Eve were happy.

God told them that everything in the garden was good for them to eat—except the fruit of one tree, the tree of the knowledge of good and evil. So when a serpent slithered up to Eve one day and encouraged her to taste the fruit of that tree, Eve knew that she was doing the only thing that God had forbidden them to do. Eve tasted the fruit and shared it with Adam.

Immediately Adam and Eve knew that what they had done was wrong. When God came to talk with them in the garden, they were ashamed and hid in the trees.

'Where are you?' God called to Adam.

'I felt guilty and afraid,' replied Adam, 'so I hid.'

'Have you eaten fruit from the tree of the knowledge of good and evil?' God asked.

'I only ate the fruit,' said

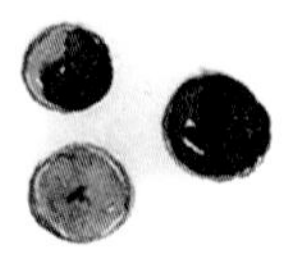

Adam. 'Eve gave it to me. It wasn't my fault.'

'What have you done?' God asked Eve.

'It was the serpent's fault,' said Eve. 'He tricked me into tasting the fruit.'

God's perfect world was perfect no more. God had given the people choice and they had chosen to do wrong. God punished the serpent: now it would crawl on its belly. He punished Eve: she would long for children but suffer pain as she gave birth to them. He punished Adam: thorns and thistles would choke the plants he grew and make his work harder.

Then God banished Adam and Eve from the beautiful garden. They now knew the difference between right and wrong. They would know suffering and death; they were no longer God's friends.

Cain and Abel

'Am I supposed to look after my brother?'

GENESIS 4:9

Adam and Eve had children, two sons called Cain and Abel.

The boys grew up and farmed the land. Cain planted seeds and grew plants they could eat, while Abel raised sheep and goats for their milk and meat.

One day Cain brought some of his crops as a gift to God, to thank him for the sun and rain and a good harvest. Abel also brought a gift of the first of his newborn lambs, to thank God that his animals had given birth safely. God saw the gifts that Cain and Abel offered him, but he also saw their motives. God accepted Abel's gift because he knew that Abel loved him and knew that all good things came from God. God was disappointed at Cain's gift, which

day. 'I am going to send a flood to wash the earth clean. You must build an ark—a huge boat that will float on the flood waters. You must take with you your wife and three sons, Shem, Ham and Japheth, and two of every kind of creature. I will keep you all safe inside the ark.'

Noah started to build the ark. It took many years of his life. God told him how long it was to be, how many decks it should have, and where to put the door. God told Noah to coat the outside with tar to make it waterproof, and to collect food for his family and all the animals. Noah did not live by the sea. The people around him watched him and laughed. They thought he was mad!

Finally, Noah's ark was finished. God told Noah to collect two of every kind of living creature, seven pairs of every kind of bird, and seven pairs of every animal that would be used for sacrifice.

THE GREAT FLOOD

... rain poured down for forty days and nights.

GENESIS 7:12

Noah began to think about how he would collect the animals together. But two by two, the animals came to Noah as if God had also told them his plan. Elephants lumbered in, snakes slithered. Birds and bats and butterflies flew through the door. Big cats padded in and deer and antelope pranced. Noah watched as the creatures filled his ark, then he went inside with his family. And God shut the door.

Slowly, steadily, persistently, the rain began to fall. It beat against the sides of the ark. It hammered on the roof. The ark began to move as the rain became a flood that lifted it high above the land, and the streams and the rivers joined into one vast expanse of sea so that no dry land was left anywhere at all.

Then one day, the rain stopped. The only sounds were inside the ark, where God kept Noah, his family and all the animals safe. Outside everything that had once lived upon the earth was destroyed by the flood.

Days passed. Weeks passed.

Months passed. Then slowly, very slowly, the waters began to go down. The ark came to rest on the Ararat mountains. Noah set free a raven but it flew back and forth until it could find food to eat. Noah set free first one dove and then another dove, until the second bird returned carrying an olive leaf in its beak.

Then God told Noah it was safe to live on the earth once more. The animals went to find new homes while Noah built an altar and sacrificed some of the birds he had brought with him to thank God for keeping them all safe.

'I will never send a flood to destroy the earth again,' promised God. 'The rainbow is a sign of my promise.'

THE PROMISED LAND

'I will bless you and make your descendants into a great nation. You will become famous and be a blessing to others.'

GENESIS 12:2

One of Noah's descendants, Terah, lived in the prosperous city of Ur of the Chaldeans. He did not worship God, but, like the people around him, worshipped a moon-god. One day, he moved to Haran with Abram and Abram's wife, Sarai, and his grandson, Lot.

God spoke to Abram just as he had spoken to Noah. And Abram also listened.

'I will show you a new land where you and your family can grow into a great nation,' God said to Abram. 'You will be set apart from other nations and I will make you into a people who live the way all people were intended to live.'

When Terah died, Abram packed up his possessions, and took with him his wife, Sarai, his nephew, Lot, and all his servants. They travelled towards the land of Canaan, pitching their tents and finding new places for their animals to feed.

Finally, they arrived in Canaan, the land that God promised would be their home. Lot chose to live in the Jordan Valley, away from Abram, so his many sheep and goats, oxen and camels, had room to grow and flourish.

Then God renewed his promise to Abram.

'This is your land. You will have so many descendants that no one will be able to count them. They will be as many as the dust in the wind and the stars in the sky. And you and your wife will have new names, Abraham and Sarah.'

Abram trusted God and was happy. He moved his tents to the great trees of Mamre at Hebron. He built an altar there and thanked God for his new home and all he had given him.

The Three Strangers

'I am the Lord! There is nothing too difficult for me.'

GENESIS 18:14

One hot day, some time later, Abraham was resting outside his tent. He saw in the distance three figures coming towards him. Abraham went to welcome the strangers. He brought water to wash their dusty feet, and offered to provide them with food to eat.

The men agreed to rest there. Abraham made sure his best calf was prepared and cooked for his visitors. Then he stood under the trees and watched while they ate their meal.

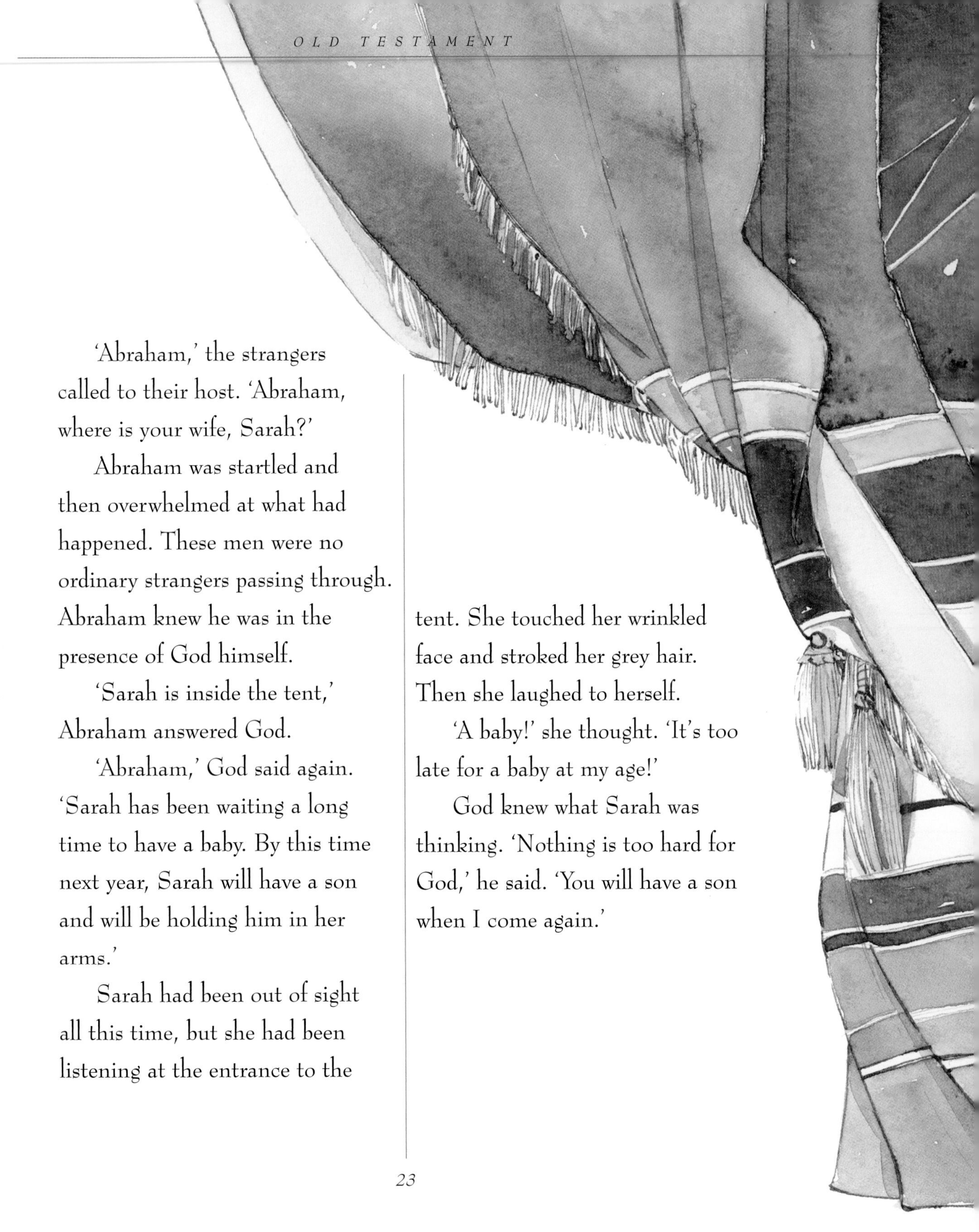

'Abraham,' the strangers called to their host. 'Abraham, where is your wife, Sarah?'

Abraham was startled and then overwhelmed at what had happened. These men were no ordinary strangers passing through. Abraham knew he was in the presence of God himself.

'Sarah is inside the tent,' Abraham answered God.

'Abraham,' God said again. 'Sarah has been waiting a long time to have a baby. By this time next year, Sarah will have a son and will be holding him in her arms.'

Sarah had been out of sight all this time, but she had been listening at the entrance to the tent. She touched her wrinkled face and stroked her grey hair. Then she laughed to herself.

'A baby!' she thought. 'It's too late for a baby at my age!'

God knew what Sarah was thinking. 'Nothing is too hard for God,' he said. 'You will have a son when I come again.'

One good man

But the Lord stayed with Abraham, who asked, 'Lord, when you destroy the evil people, are you also going to destroy those who are good?'

GENESIS 18:22–23

'It is said that terrible things happen in Sodom and Gomorrah,' God told Abraham. 'I must go there and see for myself. If it is true, then the evil there must be destroyed.'

Abraham thought about the people who lived in the cities.

'What if you find 50 good men?' Abraham asked God. 'Surely you won't destroy the city then.'

'No,' replied God. 'If I find 50 good men, it will be saved.'

'Don't be angry with me,' Abraham said. 'But what if you find 30 good men?'

'I will spare the city,' promised God.

Once more Abraham spoke. 'Twenty?'

God promised to spare the people of Sodom.

'What if you find just ten good men in the whole of the city?' asked Abraham.

'For the sake of ten good men, I will not destroy it,' said God finally.

When the strangers arrived in the city, Lot offered them hospitality. But the strangers said they would stay in the city square that night.

'Please! Come and stay with my family,' he insisted. When they finally agreed, Lot prepared a meal for them. But soon a crowd of angry men gathered outside his home.

'We know you have strangers staying with you,' they shouted. 'Send them out!'

Lot went out to calm the crowd. 'These men are under my protection,' he said. 'I cannot let you hurt them!'

'You're an outsider too,' they shouted at Lot. 'You can die along with your visitors!'

The strangers pulled Lot back inside the house. 'You must leave here quickly,' they said. 'By morning this city will be destroyed. Run! And don't look back.'

Lot escaped with his wife and daughters. God sent burning rain, so that the wicked people in Sodom and Gomorrah were destroyed. But Lot's wife looked back to see what had happened. She was turned into a pillar of salt.

ABRAHAM'S FAITH

'My son,' Abraham answered, 'God will provide the lamb.'

GENESIS 22:8

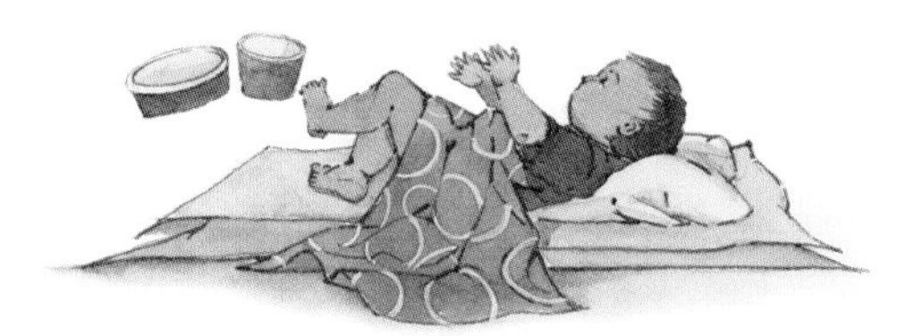

God kept his promise to Abraham and God's words to Sarah came true. Sarah gave birth to a baby son. They called him Isaac, which means 'Laughter'. Isaac grew up strong and healthy. He made both his parents very happy.

'Abraham!' God said one day. 'I want you to take Isaac with you to a mountain in Moriah. I know how much you love your son. I want you to give him back to me as a sacrifice.'

Abraham could hardly believe what he had heard. He loved God with all his heart. But he also loved his son. Then Abraham thought about how God had kept his promises in the past. He knew he trusted God.

Abraham cut wood for a fire and took Isaac with him into the mountains.

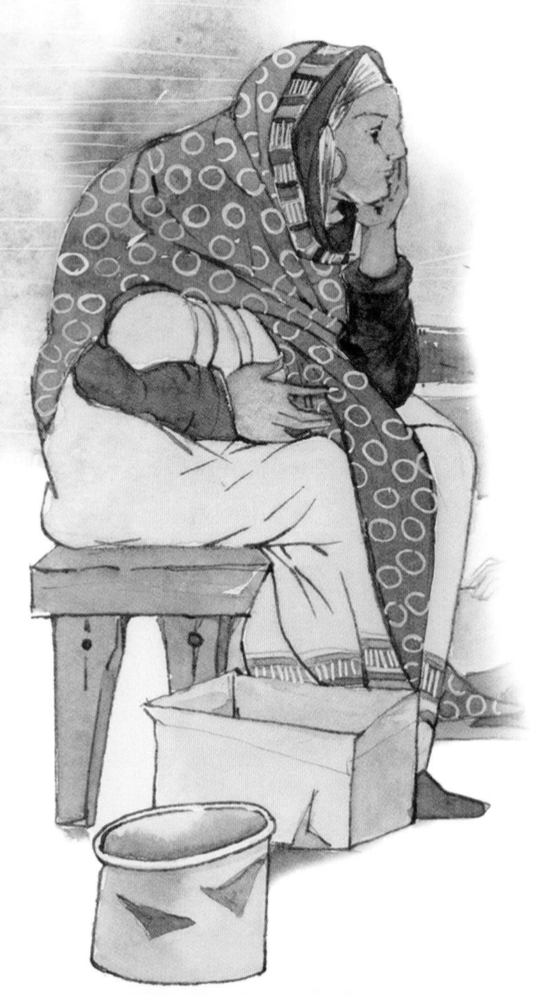

'Father,' asked Isaac, after they had walked a while in silence. 'We have brought wood for the sacrifice, but where is the lamb?'

'God will provide the lamb,' said Abraham.

Abraham laid the wood on the stones for the altar. Then he tied his son's hands and placed him on top of the wood. He could not look at Isaac's face as he lifted the knife.

'Stop!' God said. 'Abraham, you have shown me just how much you love me. You trusted me with your son, the most precious gift you had to offer. Now I will bless you, and you will have as many descendants as there are stars in the sky!'

Then Abraham saw a ram caught in a bush. God had provided the sacrifice. His son, Isaac, was safe.

TEN THIRSTY CAMELS

Rebekah became his wife. He loved her.

GENESIS 24:67

When Sarah died, Abraham knew he must find a good wife for his son, not from the Canaanites who lived near them, but a wife who would love God. So he sent his servant back across the desert to the village where his own brother lived.

The sun was setting when the servant arrived there. He made his ten camels kneel down as the women were coming from their homes to draw water.

Then the servant prayed.

'Lord God of Abraham, help me find the wife you have chosen for Isaac. Let her be the first girl who offers to draw water for me and all of these thirsty camels.'

The servant then watched a beautiful young woman come to the well. He asked her for a drink. She gave him the water and then offered to stay and draw water for all his ten camels. She returned to the well to fill her water jar again and again and again.

Abraham's servant asked the young woman who she was—and found that she was the daughter of Abraham's brother. Her name was Rebekah.

The servant was sure that God had led him to that place and that Rebekah was the right wife for Isaac. He gave her the gifts he had brought with him, a golden nose ring and two bracelets. Rebekah went home to tell her family about the man by the well, and her brother Laban came to invite him back to their home.

The servant went with him and explained that Abraham had sent him to find a wife for Isaac from his own people. God had answered his prayers by sending Rebekah to water his camels. Rebekah's family were happy when Rebekah agreed to go with him on the journey back to Canaan.

Isaac had been watching for the camels when they arrived at the place where Abraham had his tents. He went out to meet them. Rebekah became his wife and Isaac loved her.

Twin brothers

'My brother Esau is a hairy man,'
Jacob reminded her. 'And I am not.'
GENESIS 27:11

Many years later, God blessed Abraham with grandchildren, twin boys. Esau was born first, covered in red hair. Jacob was born holding on to his brother's heel. Esau grew up to be a skilled hunter and was his father's favourite son. Rebekah loved the quiet Jacob the best.

One day, Esau came home, tired from hunting, and smelled the thick lentil stew that Jacob was cooking.

'Give me some of that stew—it smells delicious!' Esau said.

'Give me your inheritance, and I will,' Jacob said. Esau was happy to agree. The food was good, and his birthright as the older son meant nothing to him.

When Isaac was old and nearly blind, he called for his eldest son, Esau, wanting to bless him before he died. Esau went out hunting to

bring his father his favourite meal. But Rebekah wanted Jacob to receive Isaac's special blessing. She prepared food for Isaac, and made Jacob dress in Esau's clothes. She tied goatskin on to his arms and neck so he would smell and feel like his hairy older brother!

When Jacob went into Isaac's tent, his father touched his son and smelled his clothes. Then he gave him his blessing.

When Esau found he had been tricked, both he and Isaac were very angry! But it was too late. The blessing had been given.

Esau brooded, determined to kill his brother, waiting only for his father's death. So Rebekah asked Isaac to send Jacob away to her brother, Laban, to find a wife from among her own people, just as Isaac had done when he married her.

JACOB'S LADDER

'Wherever you go, I will watch over you.'

GENESIS 28:15

Jacob left his family and began his journey to Haran, where his uncle Laban lived.

When it was night, Jacob lay down to sleep, with a stone for a pillow. Then Jacob dreamed. In his dream he saw a long flight of steps like a ladder, stretching from the earth where he slept into the heavens above him. Moving up and down the ladder, Jacob saw beautiful angels, and at the very top, God himself.

Then Jacob heard God's voice speaking to him.

'I am the God of your father, Isaac, and your grandfather, Abraham. I promise I will give to you and your descendants the land you are now lying on. I will watch over you, Jacob, and I will never leave you.'

When Jacob awoke, he was afraid. He knew that he had seen

God—and he had lived. He took the stone he had used as a pillow and stood it up like a pillar to mark the special place. Then Jacob made God a promise too.

'If you look after me as you have promised, dear God, I will obey you and follow you always,' he said.

As Jacob walked on towards Haran, he saw in the distance some shepherds and their sheep waiting by a large well. When he reached them he was pleased to find that they came from Haran, and told them that his Uncle Laban lived there too.

'Laban?' one shepherd asked him. 'That's Rachel, Laban's daughter, over there.'

When Jacob looked at the woman they pointed to, he saw a beautiful shepherdess leading her sheep towards the well. Jacob went to meet Rachel and brought water for her sheep. When he told her that he was her cousin, she was so pleased, she ran back to tell her father, and Laban welcomed Jacob into his family.

ABRAHAM'S DESCENDANTS

'I will give you the land that I promised Abraham and Isaac, and it will belong to your family for ever.'

GENESIS 35:12

Jacob stayed with his uncle. He ate with the family and he worked with the family. After a month, Laban asked Jacob what payment he wanted. Jacob had been with Laban only a short time, but he knew that he had fallen in love with the beautiful shepherdess he had first seen. Jacob asked if he could marry Rachel.

'If you will allow us to marry, I will work for you for seven years,' said Jacob.

Laban agreed and Jacob reared and cared for his sheep and his goats, knowing that Rachel would one day be his wife.

When the time came, Laban prepared a feast to celebrate his daughter's marriage to Jacob. But when the wedding took place, Laban made Rachel's older sister, Leah, dress in bridal garments with her face covered by a veil. Jacob was married not to Rachel, but to Leah, Laban's eldest daughter. Jacob, who had once tricked his brother, had now been tricked himself!

'We agreed that I would work for Rachel, not for Leah!' he said when he found out.

'This is our custom, for the

elder daughter to be married first,' replied Laban. 'But I will let you marry Rachel now, and have both women, if you will work for me for another seven years.'

Jacob loved Rachel very much. He agreed to care for both wives.

As time passed, Jacob had many children: Reuben, Simeon, Levi, Judah, Issachar, Zebulun, Dinah, Dan, Naphtali, Gad, Asher and Joseph. Joseph was Rachel's only child. Jacob loved Joseph the best.

Twenty years had passed while Jacob had been with his Uncle Laban. It was time to move back to Canaan. He took with him his wives and children and all the spotted or speckled sheep and goats from Laban's herds. Rachel gave him his last child, Benjamin, before she died.

God had blessed him. Now he changed Jacob's name to Israel.

Jacob's Favourite Son

Jacob loved Joseph more than he did any of his other sons, because Joseph was born after Jacob was very old.

GENESIS 37:3

By the time he was 17, Joseph knew that he was Jacob's favourite son. Joseph helped his brothers to look after his father's flocks. But Joseph watched them and listened to them, and then told his father the bad things they said and did.

Jacob gave Joseph a beautiful, long-sleeved, many-coloured coat. When Joseph's brothers saw it, they knew that he was loved much more than they were—and they hated him.

One night, Joseph had a strange dream.

'I dreamed we were all binding bundles of corn. My bundle stood up straight, and yours bowed down before mine!' The brothers made angry faces behind Joseph's back!

Then Joseph had another strange dream.

'I dreamed that the sun, the moon and eleven stars all bowed down before me!'

Jacob was unhappy. But he wondered whether the dreams were sent from God.

Some time later Jacob sent Joseph to find out how his brothers were. They were grazing the sheep and goats miles from home. His brothers saw him coming, dressed in his beautiful coat—and plotted to kill him!

As soon as Joseph reached them, the brothers pulled off his coat and forced him down into an empty well. But then they saw a way to make money out of their brother. Some Midianites were passing by on their way to Egypt to trade spices. The brothers dragged Joseph out of the well and sold him for 20 pieces of silver.

The last they saw of their brother was as he was taken away to Egypt to be sold as a slave. The men then killed one of their goats and dipped Joseph's coat in the blood. They needed a story for their father.

'Look what we have found!' they told Jacob.

Jacob assumed that Joseph had been attacked by a wild animal. He was overcome with grief. His favourite son must surely be dead.

Dreams in Egypt

The Lord was helping Joseph to be successful in whatever he did.

GENESIS 39:2

Joseph's brothers had abandoned him. But God had not.

Joseph was sold to Potiphar, the captain of the guard. God blessed Joseph and soon Potiphar trusted him with everything he owned. Joseph became Potiphar's chief servant. But Joseph was a strong, good-looking young man and soon Potiphar's wife wanted him for herself. When he began to avoid her, she became so angry that she lied about him and Joseph was thrown into prison.

Now Potiphar had abandoned Joseph. But still God had not. God blessed him again, and soon he was put in charge of the other prisoners. So he was in the right place at the right time

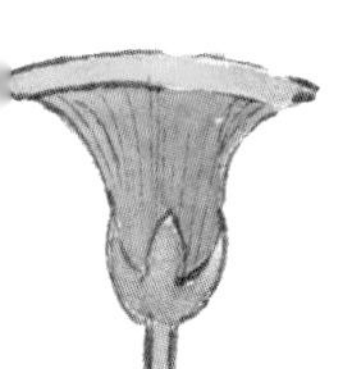

when Pharaoh's personal servant and chief cook were also put in prison—and dreamed strange dreams. Joseph told the cook that he would be executed, but the personal servant was forgiven and given back his job.

But then the personal servant abandoned Joseph. Two more years passed—until Pharaoh started to have strange dreams too.

'There is a man in your prison who can help,' the servant remembered.

So Joseph was brought out of prison, cleaned up and told the dreams. Joseph asked God to help him understand them. Then he told Pharaoh what would happen.

'In the first dream, seven thin cows ate up seven fat, healthy cows,' said Joseph. 'In the second dream, seven thin, straggly ears of corn swallowed up seven healthy ears of corn.

God is warning you that there will be seven years of good harvest followed by seven years of famine. If you store the grain wisely, you and your people will survive.'

Pharaoh put Joseph in charge immediately so the grain could be stored carefully. He put a ring on Joseph's finger, a gold chain around his neck and dressed him in fine clothes. Wherever Joseph went in the land of Egypt, people bowed down to him.

God had not abandoned Joseph. His dreams began to come true.

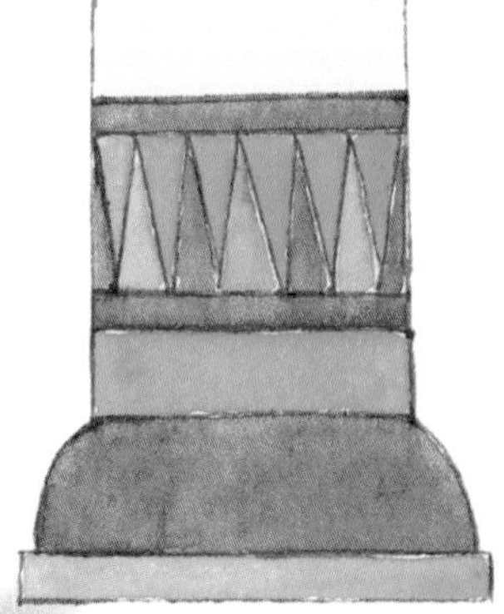

God's plan for Jacob's family

'After all, you weren't really the ones who sent me here—it was God.'

GENESIS 45:8

Joseph made sure that all the grain in the abundant harvests was stored carefully. Then, as the harvests failed in Egypt and in all the lands around them, Joseph opened the storehouses and sold the grain to the Egyptians. Everyone had what they needed to survive the famine.

In Canaan Jacob heard that people were travelling to buy grain from Egypt. He sent ten of his sons to buy some, keeping only Benjamin at home with him.

Jacob's sons went to the Egyptian governor and bowed down before him. None of the brothers recognised their lost brother Joseph in the man before them. But Joseph knew who they were.

Joseph used an interpreter so they would not know he understood their language. Then he tested them to see if they had changed from the men who had almost killed their brother; from the men who had sold him into slavery. When Joseph saw that they were sorry and would do anything rather than hurt their father again, he showed them who he was.

'I am your brother, Joseph,' he told them. 'You wished me harm, but God meant only that good should come of it. God made sure I was here in Egypt so that your lives could be saved. Go back to your father and mine. Tell him

that I am governor of all Egypt and that it is safe for him to come here. You will live in the land of Goshen with your families and all that you own; and you will have plenty to eat during the famine.'

So Jacob left the land of Canaan and took his children and grandchildren with him to live in Egypt. He was reunited with Joseph and was happy. God had blessed them all.

MOSES AND THE PRINCESS OF EGYPT

Many years later a new king came to power. He did not know what Joseph had done for Egypt.

EXODUS 1:8

Pharaohs came and went. A time came when Joseph had died and the land of Egypt was full of his descendants. A new Pharaoh looked at the Israelites and was afraid of their great numbers.

The Egyptians made the Israelites work hard for them and ill-treated them. But God blessed them. Pharaoh ordered the midwives to kill all baby boys born to the Israelite women. The midwives told him that the women were strong and gave birth before they arrived to help. So God blessed the Egyptian midwives. Then Pharaoh gave an order that all baby boys must be thrown into the Nile and drowned.

At least one Israelite woman would not let that happen.

Jochebed hid her baby son until he was three months old. When he was too big to hide any longer, she put him in a basket, coated it with tar to make it waterproof, and told her daughter, Miriam, to hide it in the reeds along the bank of the River Nile.

Pharaoh's daughter heard the sound of a baby crying when she came to the river to bathe. She felt sorry for him.

'Shall I find someone to nurse him for you?' asked Miriam, who was watching nearby.

'Yes,' said the princess. 'I will keep this baby and call him Moses.'

Miriam went to fetch her mother. So it was that Jochebed looked after her baby under the protection of an Egyptian princess.

And when Moses was old enough, he went to live with the princess. He grew up in the palace as if he were an Egyptian.

The Burning Bush

Moses was afraid to look at God, and so he hid his face.

EXODUS 3:6

One day, Moses watched the sweat dripping from the brows of the Israelite slaves. Then he saw an Egyptian beating one of his own people. Moses was angry. He made sure that no one was watching him, then he killed the Egyptian and buried him in the sand.

The next day, Moses saw two Israelites fighting and asked them why.

'Why do you care?' one of them replied. 'Will you kill me as you killed the Egyptian?'

Moses realised that someone had seen him after all. He fled. He made his home in Midian, and married Zipporah, one of Jethro's seven daughters.

Moses was looking after Jethro's sheep one day when he saw a bush that seemed to be on fire. Moving closer, he saw that the flames did not destroy the leaves but from them a voice called his name.

'Here I am,' he replied.

An angel of the Lord told Moses to take off his shoes. The ground he stood on was holy. Moses was so afraid, he hid his face. Then God spoke to him.

'I am the God of Abraham, the God of Isaac and the God of

Jacob. I have seen how my people are suffering as slaves in Egypt. I want them to be free to live in the land I have promised them. Go to Pharaoh. Bring my people out of Egypt.'

'But I can't!' said Moses. 'Why would Pharaoh listen to me?'

'I will help you,' replied God.

Then God showed Moses signs that would help him convince Pharaoh that he had been sent by God. God turned Moses' stick into a snake, then turned it back again. He made Moses' hand become white with leprosy—then healed it again. God told him to pour out a cup of water from the Nile—and it would turn to blood.

Moses was still afraid. He feared he did not speak well.

'I made you,' said God. 'I know all about you. I can help you with everything I have asked you to do. But you may take your brother, Aaron, with you to speak on your behalf.'

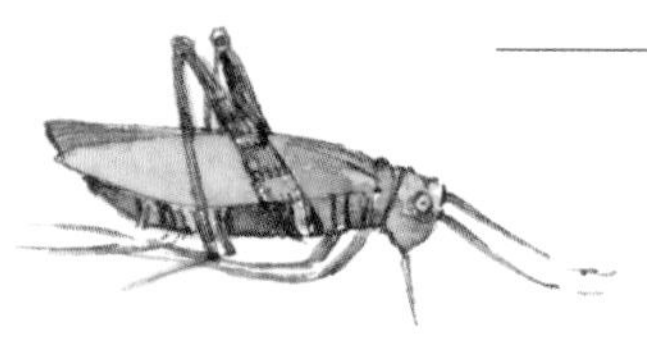

PLAGUES IN EGYPT

'The Lord God says: "Let my people go."'

EXODUS 5:1

Moses and Aaron went to see Pharaoh.

'We have come with a message from the Lord, the God of Israel. "Let my people go, so that they can worship me,"' they said.

'I don't know your God,' said Pharaoh, 'and I don't want to let the Israelites go. They are slaves, and I need them to work. I will not let them go!'

Then Pharaoh gave new orders to his slave-drivers, so that the Israelites would have to gather their own straw to make bricks and therefore work even harder than before.

Moses and Aaron went to see Pharaoh again.

'The Lord, the God of Israel says, "Let my people go!"'

Just as before, Pharaoh refused to let the Israelites go.

So God sent plagues to Egypt.

First the water in the River Nile turned to blood. All the fish died. The smell was terrible! But Pharaoh refused to let the people go.

Next there was a plague of frogs. The frogs were everywhere,

inside the houses and all over the land. Pharaoh agreed to let the people go, but then he changed his mind.

Seven more times Moses and Aaron asked Pharaoh to let the Israelites go. When Pharaoh refused, God sent plagues of gnats, flies and locusts; every Egyptian animal died, and the people were covered in boils; violent hailstorms battered the land, and finally, the whole of Egypt was plunged into darkness.

After each plague Pharaoh agreed to let the Israelites go, but as soon as God took away the plague, Pharaoh changed his mind.

Then God told Moses that he would send one more plague. The firstborn of every living creature in Egypt would die—but God would protect his people. Still Pharaoh would not let the people go.

That night every Israelite family coated their door frames with lamb's blood so that the angel of death would pass over them. They ate roast lamb with unleavened bread and herbs, dressed in their cloaks and sandals, ready to leave quickly.

Then the cries of the Egyptians could be heard throughout the land. God had sent the tenth and final plague.

Crossing the Red Sea

'Don't be afraid! Be brave, and you will see the Lord save you today.'

EXODUS 14:13

Pharaoh told Moses and Aaron to take their people, their cattle and sheep and leave the land of Egypt. The Egyptians even gave the Israelites gold and silver—as long as they would go.

Then God led his people to the land of Canaan. By day God appeared as a pillar of cloud and by night God was a pillar of fire. God led them by the desert road towards the Red Sea.

But soon Pharaoh changed his mind again. He began to regret that he had let his slaves go. He took 600 of his best chariots and every other chariot he could find in Egypt; he took horses, horsemen and troops on foot and pursued the Israelites.

When the Israelites saw the dust of the chariots behind them, they were very afraid.

'Were there no graves in Egypt?' they asked Moses. 'Have you brought us here into the desert to die?'

But Moses was not afraid. He knew that God would save his people.

Moses stretched out his hand over the Red Sea. God sent a wind to blow back the waters so that all the Israelites could pass safely

to the other side on dry land. The Egyptians started to follow, but Moses stretched out his hand again and God sent back the water. Pharaoh and his army and chariots were covered with the waters of the Red Sea.

When Moses and the Israelites saw what had happened, they sang and danced to thank God for saving them from years of suffering.

'Our God is great and mighty! He threw horses and riders into the sea. Our God is strong and mighty! He came to rescue us all. He came for us as he promised. He loves us and leads us. Sing to the Lord God! He is the greatest!'

The Ten Commandments

'I am the Lord your God, the one who brought you out of Egypt where you were slave.'

EXODUS 20:2

Moses led the Israelites across the desert beyond the sea.

When they needed water, God made the water sweet. When they were hungry, God made manna fall from the sky like rain and sent quail for them to eat. The manna looked like frost and tasted like wafers made from honey. God made sure they had enough for two days at the end of the week so they could rest on the seventh day, the Sabbath.

After three months in the desert, the Israelites camped at the foot of Mount Sinai. God spoke to Moses.

'I saved you from the Egyptians and brought you safely across the Red Sea,' said God. 'Now I will make a promise to you: if you will obey me and keep your side of the agreement, you will be my special people and I will be your God.'

The Israelites agreed to obey God. They wanted to be his special people. So God called Moses to the top of the mountain to give him rules so that his people could live together in peace. God engraved them on two stone tablets, in his own hand.

'I am the Lord your God, who brought you out of Egypt where you were slaves. Do not worship any god but me.

'Do not make idols that look like anything in the sky or on the earth or in the ocean under the earth. Don't bow down and worship idols.

'Do not misuse my name. I am the Lord your God.

'Remember that the Sabbath day belongs to me. You have six days to do your work, but the seventh day belongs to me, your God. No one is to work on that day.

'Respect your father and your mother, and you will live a long time in the land I am giving you.

'Do not murder.

'Be faithful in marriage.

'Do not steal.

'Do not tell lies about others.

'Do not desire anything that belongs to someone else. Don't desire anyone's house, wife or husband, slaves, oxen, donkeys or anything else.'

God also told Moses how he wanted the people to worship him. When God had finished talking to Moses, he gave him the two stone tablets and Moses took them down the mountain.

Forty years in the desert

'Will you choose for the Lord to make you prosperous and give you a long life? Or will he put you under a curse and kill you? Choose life!'

DEUTERONOMY 30:19

God promised the Israelites a land flowing with milk and honey, rich and fertile, where they could live in peace and worship him. As they approached Canaan, God told Moses to send one man from each of the twelve families or tribes to explore the Promised Land.

When they returned, Caleb and Joshua carried between them a pole with a heavy branch bearing juicy grapes. They also brought figs and pomegranates. The land would be a wonderful place to live. But the other ten spies were less happy.

'We saw people as big as giants, living in walled cities!' they warned.

Then the Israelites wanted to go back to Egypt.

'But God has promised to give us this wonderful land. We can trust him!' said Moses.

The people would not listen. So God let those who would not enter the land he had given them wander in the desert for 40 years. Only their children and the two spies who trusted God would enter the Promised Land.

Before he died, Moses spoke

to the people one last time.

'Help the poor. If you share what you have and are generous to one another you will have abundant harvests and plenty of water. The nations around you will see that God has blessed you. But you must love God and keep his commandments. God has given you a choice between life or death. Choose life, and live for a long time in the land he will give you.'

Moses called Joshua to him and laid his hands on him in front of all the people.

'Be strong and brave, Joshua. God has chosen you to lead his people into the Promised Land.'

RAHAB HIDES THE SPIES

'We know that the Lord your God rules heaven and earth.'

JOSHUA 2:11

Joshua and the Israelites were camped on one side of the River Jordan. On the other side was the city of Jericho, with walls thick and tall.

Joshua sent spies into the city. Secretly they made their way to a house built into the city walls. They talked to Rahab, the woman who lived there, and found out about the people who lived in Jericho. But the spies had not been careful enough. The king of Jericho was told that Rahab was talking to Israelite spies. He sent a message for her to hand them over.

Rahab quickly hid the spies under the flax drying on her roof. She told the king that the spies had already gone and had left by the city gate. The king's men hurried out in pursuit of the Israelites.

When it was safe, Rahab went to the men hiding on her roof and made a bargain with them.

'You are well known to the people here. They know that your God dried up the waters of the Red Sea. They know he saved you from slavery in Egypt. They know that he is with you now and will give this city to you. God is on your side and we are all afraid. So—help me now. Promise that you will save my family when you capture the city.'

The spies agreed. They told her to bring her whole family to the room and to hang a scarlet cord from her window in the city wall when the Israelites came into the city. They would not be harmed.

So Rahab helped the spies escape through the window and down the city walls, to hide in the hills.

Crossing the River Jordan

'Don't ever be afraid or discouraged! I am the Lord your God, and I will be with you wherever you go.'

JOSHUA 1:9

Joshua listened to the news brought back by the spies. Now he knew that the people of Jericho feared for their lives. God had promised to help them, and God would keep his promise. But Joshua still had to cross the River Jordan with all the Israelites.

God encouraged Joshua.

'Today, everyone will know that I am here to help you, just as I helped Moses. Don't be afraid. Trust me. I will not let you down.' Then God gave Joshua instructions on how he would lead the people into the Promised Land by crossing the River Jordan. Joshua did exactly what God told him to do.

First the priests stepped into the river, carrying the sacred chest, which contained the two stones with the Ten Commandments written on them. As soon as they did so, the waters that ran downstream stopped flowing. The priests stayed in the middle of the river, and the Israelites—men,

women and children—crossed on dry land. Then one man from each of the twelve tribes took a rock from the middle of the river bed, and they placed them on the other side of the river to mark what God had done for them. When all the people had crossed the river, the priests carrying the sacred chest walked to the other side too. Only then did the waters of the River Jordan flow again.

No one wanted to fight against the Israelites after this. Everyone in Canaan heard how God had crossed thousands of people safely across the River Jordan.

THE BATTLE OF JERICHO

The Lord helped Joshua in everything he did,
and Joshua was famous everywhere in Canaan.

JOSHUA 6:27

Joshua camped with all the Israelites outside the city walls of Jericho. Together they ate the special Passover meal that celebrated the time when God freed them from slavery in Egypt. And from that time on they did not need the manna that God had sent them from heaven. Then they waited until God told them what to do next.

Suddenly a man with a sword in his hand appeared in Joshua's path. Joshua knew that God had sent him, and fell to his knees.

'I am the commander of God's army,' said the man. 'I will tell you what you must do. Seven priests must lead you in a march around the city walls. The priests

must walk in front of the sacred chest, each carrying a trumpet, for six days. On the seventh day, they must march around the city walls seven times, blowing their trumpets. On the long trumpet blast, signal the people to shout. Then the city walls will collapse in front of you.'

The gates of the city of Jericho stood before Joshua and his army, firmly closed against them. The people inside the city watched and waited to see what the Israelites would do.

Joshua led God's people. For six days they marched as God had told them. On the seventh day, at the sound of the long trumpet blast, the people shouted and the walls of Jericho crumbled and fell down.

The Israelites marched into the city. They found Rahab and all her family and kept them safe just as they had promised, because she had hidden the spies and believed that God was with them.

God had given them the victory. The Israelites were in the Promised Land.

DEBORAH, THE WISE JUDGE

'The Lord has already gone on ahead to fight for you.'

JUDGES 4:14

Many years passed. Sometimes the Israelites loved God and followed his commandments. When they forgot him, and worshipped other gods and neglected the poor, they were oppressed by the people who lived in Canaan.

King Jabin had a large and fierce army. His commander, Sisera, had 900 iron chariots, and for 20 years he made life miserable for the Israelites, until finally they begged the Lord for help.

A prophet named Deborah led Israel at this time. She loved God, and when God heard the prayers of his people, he told Deborah what to do. Deborah sent for Barak, a great soldier.

'God has a job for you, Barak. You must march 10,000 men to Mount Tabor. Sisera and King Jabin's army will go to the River Kishon and be trapped there. Then you can defeat them.'

Barak listened to Deborah, but he was frightened.

'I can't do this,' he said. 'I want you to come with me.'

Deborah was sad that Barak did not trust God. But she agreed

to go with him.

'There will be a victory today, Barak, but it will be given to a woman, not to you!'

When Sisera heard that Barak was leading an attack, he gathered his army and 900 chariots by the river. Barak went up to Mount Tabor with his troops and waited for Deborah's signal. As he attacked, God confused Sisera, his chariot drivers and his whole army. Everyone was afraid of Barak and his army.

Sisera fled from the battle scene and looked for somewhere to hide. A woman called Jael saw Sisera and offered to provide shelter for him.

'Don't be afraid,' she said. 'No one will find you here in my tent.'

Jael gave him some milk to drink and covered him up so no one could see him. Then, exhausted, Sisera fell asleep.

But Jael was on God's side. While Sisera was sleeping she drove a tent peg through his head.

When Barak came looking for Sisera, Jael showed him the dead man, killed by a woman, just as Deborah had prophesied.

'Praise God!' sang Deborah and Barak. 'He has saved us from our enemies.'

GIDEON'S SHEEPSKIN

Then once again the Israelites started disobeying the Lord.

JUDGES 6:1

There was peace for 40 years—until once more the Israelites forgot what God had done for them. This time the Midianites made their lives miserable. They waited until the Israelites had grown their crops, then swooped down on their camels and spoiled the land or stole what they had grown. The Israelites were weak from hunger. They hid in the mountains and lived in fear for seven years.

Then they remembered God and prayed. God sent Gideon to help them.

Gideon was hiding from the Midianites, threshing wheat, when God sent an angel to tell him that he had been chosen to help his people.

'God is with you, mighty warrior!' the angel said to Gideon. 'God wants you to save Israel from the Midianites.'

'But why me?' Gideon replied. 'I am no one! I belong to the smallest clan in my tribe; I am the least in my family!'

'God will help you,' said the angel. 'You will not be alone.'

'I need a sign, to prove that I am not dreaming! I will put a sheepskin on the ground this evening. In the morning, if the sheepskin is wet and the ground dry, I will know that you want me to lead Israel.'

In the morning Gideon squeezed the sheepskin. It was wet, but the ground all around was dry.

'Please don't be angry with me, Lord, but I must be sure. Let me put the sheepskin out again, only this time, let the ground be wet and the sheepskin dry.'

In the morning the ground was covered with dew, and the sheepskin was dry. God had answered Gideon. Now he was ready to help God's people and lead them against their enemies.

The trumpet in the night

The Lord said, 'Gideon, your army is too big.
I can't let you win with this many soldiers.'

JUDGES 7:2

Gideon gathered all the fighting men.

But the army was too big.

'You have too many soldiers,' God told Gideon. 'When the battle is won, the Israelites will believe they did it all themselves. Send home anyone who is afraid.'

Many men were afraid! That day, 22,000 men went home.

'There are still too many,' said God. 'Send the men to the river to drink.'

Some of the men knelt down at the water, while others lapped the water out of their hands.

'I will use the men who lapped the water,' said God. 'Send the others home.'

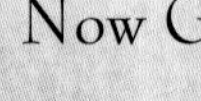

Now Gideon had an army of just 300 men to fight against the Midianites.

Then God told Gideon to go down to the enemy camp in the dead of night and listen to what the soldiers were saying. Gideon saw tens of thousands of men—and more camels than grains of sand on the seashore.

'I've had a horrible dream!'

Gideon heard one man tell another. 'A huge, round barley loaf rolled into our camp. It hit the tent so violently, it collapsed!'

'But that means God is on Gideon's side!' said another. 'They will win this battle!'

Gideon crept back to his own camp, silently thanking God for what he had heard.

'Come! God has already won the battle for us!' he told his men.

Gideon divided his men into three groups. He gave each man a trumpet and a burning torch covered by an empty jar. Then the Israelites surounded the enemy camp while it was still night. At Gideon's signal, he and his men blew their trumpets and smashed the jars.

'For the Lord and for Gideon!' they cried.

The Midianites were terrified! They stumbled and fell upon each other in the darkness. They killed each other with their swords, not knowing where their enemy was.

Everything happened as God had promised. God had once more saved his people.

Samson, the Strong Man

'Very soon you will be pregnant and have a son. He will belong to God from the day he is born.'

JUDGES 13:5

Time passed and the Israelites returned once more to their old ways. The Philistines took control of them and ruled over them for 40 years.

God sent an angel to a woman

who could have no children, the wife of a man called Manoah.

'Don't be afraid. God will bless you with a baby son who will save Israel from the Philistines. His life will be dedicated to God.'

When the woman gave birth to a son, she called him Samson, and God blessed the child.

When Samson grew up, he wanted to marry a Philistine woman. Before the wedding, a young lion bounded towards him and tried to attack him. God gave Samson amazing strength. He fought with the lion and killed it with his bare hands. But Samson told no one what had happened. When Samson returned to the place some time later, bees had nested in the lion's carcass. Samson found honey inside. So during the wedding feast, Samson told the Philistines a riddle.

'Once so strong and mighty—now so sweet and tasty! If you can tell me the answer to my riddle within seven days, I will give you a prize. But if not, you must reward me.'

The Philistines could not answer the riddle, but they would not give in to an Israelite. They secretly threatened Samson's new wife to find out the answer. The woman cried and begged until Samson told her the answer and she in turn told the Philistines. The Philistines answered Samson: 'What is sweeter than honey? What is stronger than a lion?'

Samson was furious. He knew he had been deceived and returned to his father's house in a rage. His father-in-law then gave Samson's wife to another man.

When Samson found out, he set fire to the Philistines' cornfields. Then with the strength God had given him, he used the jaw bone of a donkey to kill a thousand of his enemies.

Defeat of the Philistines

'Please remember me, Lord God... Make me strong one last time.'

JUDGES 16:28

The Philistines hated Samson. But they also feared his enormous strength.

When Samson fell in love with a woman called Delilah, the Philistines offered her bribes so that she would betray the secret of his amazing strength.

Night after night she would ask him, 'Tell me the secret of your strength.'

Samson found this amusing at first and he teased her with false answers. Delilah tied him with seven new bowstrings, then with new ropes. She wove his long braided hair on to a loom. But when she tested him, Samson still had his strength.

'If you really love me, you will tell me,' she said.

Eventually Samson could stand it no longer. He told Delilah his secret.

'My hair has never been cut,' he told her. 'If my head is shaved, I will lose my strength.'

So when Samson slept, his hair was shaved off. Then when Delilah told him the Philistines were there to capture him, his strength was the same as any other man. He was taken prisoner, blinded and put in prison.

The Philistines celebrated their victory over Samson. They brought him out to taunt him. All the Philistine rulers were in the temple, with 3000 people on the roof.

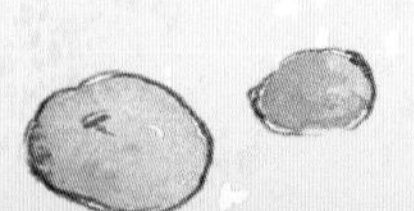
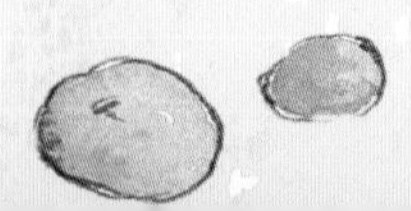

Samson asked the servant who guided him to put him between the pillars of the temple. Then he stretched out his arms.

'Help me defeat my enemies, Lord God,' prayed Samson. 'Give me strength just one more time and let me die as I have lived, by destroying the Philistines.'

Samson pushed at the pillars with all his might and God answered his prayer. The giant pillars cracked, pulling the walls inwards and bringing the roof crashing to the ground. Samson had destroyed the Philistine temple, and with it, thousands of Philistines. He had killed by his death more of his enemies than in his lifetime.

Ruth and Boaz

'I will go where you go, I will live where you live; your people will be my people, your God will be my God.'

RUTH 1:16

There was a famine in Israel. Elimelech took his wife Naomi to live in Moab. His sons, Mahlon and Kilion, married there.

Elimelech died in Moab. Mahlon and Kilion died too and the three women were left alone. When Naomi decided to return to her home near Bethlehem, she encouraged her daughters-in-law to stay behind. But Ruth would not leave Naomi.

'Your people will become my people and your God will become my God. I will go where you go, die where you die, and be buried there.'

So Ruth and Naomi went to Bethlehem.

'I will go and pick up the leftover grain in the fields, so we can eat,' Ruth told Naomi.

God blessed Ruth, and she found herself working in the fields belonging to Boaz, a relative of Elimelech. She worked hard, and when Boaz found that she had been good to Naomi, he was kind to her. He made sure she collected enough grain to stop them being hungry.

Naomi saw that Boaz was kind to Ruth. At that time were was a custom that if a man died leaving a young wife a relative should marry her to care for his family. Boaz agreed to look after Ruth and Naomi. When he had made sure that no other relative wanted to marry Ruth, he arranged their wedding day.

Boaz was happy. He married Ruth and God blessed them all. Some time later, Naomi found herself not only in Boaz's household but proudly holding her first grandson.

'I lost my husband and both my sons, but God gave me Ruth, who has looked after me as if she were my own daughter. Now I have my grandson, Obed, too. God has blessed me,' said Naomi.

Obed grew up to have a son called Jesse, who himself had eight sons. The youngest boy was called David.

HANNAH KEEPS HER PROMISE

'I... asked the Lord to give me a child. Here he is! The Lord gave me just what I asked for.'

1 SAMUEL 1:26–27

Elkanah and his two wives, Hannah and Peninnah, went to Shiloh every year to worship God. Peninnah had many children but Hannah had none. One year, Hannah went to the place of worship and wept.

'Lord God,' she prayed, 'if you will bless me with a baby son, then I will let him serve you all his life.'

Hannah told Eli, the priest, that she was praying about her problems.

'May God bless you and answer your prayer,' he said.

God did answer Hannah's prayer. Some time later she gave birth to baby Samuel.

Hannah loved her son very much. But Hannah kept her promise. She looked after Samuel until he was old enough to leave her, then she took him to Shiloh.

'God answered my prayers,' she told Eli. 'Now my son must learn how to serve God.'

Samuel became Eli's helper. As Eli's eyes became weak, he came to depend on Samuel.

One night, when everyone was asleep, God called to Samuel.

Samuel woke at the sound of the voice but he did not know who it was. He got up and went to Eli.

'Here I am!' said Samuel. 'You called me!'

'No, I didn't call,' said Eli. 'Go back to sleep.'

Before long Samuel heard the voice calling him again.

'Samuel! Samuel!' God called.

He went again to Eli.

'I didn't call you,' said Eli. 'Go back to your bed.'

Then Samuel heard the voice for a third time. This time Eli understood who was calling him.

'God is calling you,' said Eli. 'This time, if the voice calls your name, reply, "Speak, Lord, for your servant is listening."'

God called Samuel again and he answered. Then God told Samuel of his plans for his people. Eli and all the people saw that Samuel was the prophet that God had sent to help them.

The first king of Israel

'Now we want a king to be our leader, just like all the other nations.'

1 SAMUEL 8:5

When Samuel was an old man, the Israelites demanded a king.

'We want to be like all the other nations!' they said. 'Choose one for us!'

Samuel knew that this was not God's way for his people, but he prayed.

'The people are rejecting me,' said God. 'A king cannot bring them what they want; they are just as stubborn as their ancestors before them. They can have a king to rule over them, but he will bring them great unhappiness.'

Samuel warned the people, but they refused to listen.

God told Samuel who would be the first king of Israel. When Samuel saw the tall, handsome young man walking towards him, he knew that Saul was the man God had chosen.

'We are looking for God's prophet,' Saul said. 'Do you know where we can find him?'

'You have found him,' Samuel answered. 'Come and eat with me. Tomorrow I have something important to tell you. And you can stop worrying about your father's lost donkeys: they have been found.'

Saul knew that this must be God's prophet—because he already knew about the donkeys he was looking for. The following day, Samuel told Saul to let his servant go on ahead so he could talk to him alone. Then Samuel anointed Saul with oil. He would be the first king of Israel.

'God will give you the power to be the person who will be able to rule Israel. Don't be afraid. God will help you.'

Saul returned to his family with the lost donkeys but he told no one about God's plans for him until Samuel called all the people together to give them their king.

Samuel went through the twelve tribes of Israel until Benjamin was chosen; he went through all the families until the family of Kish was chosen and then he came to Saul, his son.

'Long live the king!' shouted God's people when Samuel presented their new leader to them. The Israelites had what they had asked for: a king like the other nations.

Jesse's youngest son

'He isn't the one I've chosen. People judge others by what they look like, but I judge people by what is in their hearts.

1 SAMUEL 16:7

Saul was a good king at first. He led the people in battle. He won victories for them. But soon he stopped relying on God to help him. He did what he wanted even when it was the opposite of what God told him to do. He gave in when the people wanted to take plunder from his enemies. Samuel shook his head sadly.

'God wants you to be obedient, not to offer him sacrifices!' Samuel told him. 'God has told me that you cannot be his king on your own. If you reject his help, he will reject you as king.'

Then Samuel waited to see what God would do next.

'Fill your horn with oil,' said God one day. 'I have chosen the man who will be king after Saul. Go to Bethlehem. Invite Jesse to a feast.'

Samuel went to Bethlehem and held a feast for the people. When he saw Jesse's eldest son, he felt sure that he must be God's choice as king. But God said no.

'I have not chosen him, Samuel. You can see only what a person looks like on the outside. I can see what is inside their heart.'

Then Samuel met Jesse's second son. But he was not the one God had chosen either.

When Samuel had met seven of Jesse's sons, and none of them was the one God had chosen, Samuel asked whether Jesse had any more sons.

'Yes, there is my youngest son, David. He is looking after my sheep,' replied Jesse.

So they sent for David and brought him to the feast.

'This is the man I have chosen to be king,' God told Samuel. 'Anoint him.'

The giant's challenge

'The Lord has rescued me from the claws of lions and bears, and he will keep me safe from the hands of this Philistine.'

1 SAMUEL 17:37

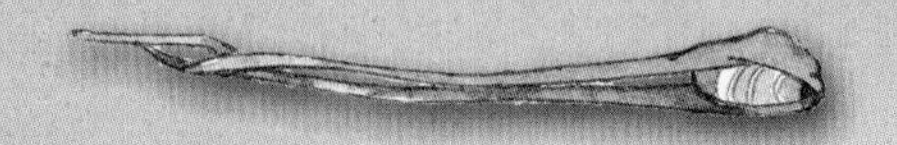

Now that God had stopped blessing Saul, the king suffered bad moods and was often depressed and angry.

His servants offered to find someone to play soothing music to calm him and when Saul agreed, they brought David, Jesse's son, to play his harp. David made up songs and sang them when he played.

'The Lord is my shepherd. I will never be in need.

'You let me rest in fields of green grass.

'You lead me to streams of peaceful water.'

One day, David saw that the Israelite battle line had gathered on one hill and the Philistines on the other. In the valley between them, the Philistine champion, a giant of a man named Goliath, marched up and down, challenging the Israelities to send out a man to fight him.

Goliath wore a bronze helmet on his head and bronze armour to protect his body and his thick legs. He carried a bronze javelin and a spear with a heavy iron point.

'How dare he challenge us!' said David to the men around him. 'We have the living God on our side.'

The Israelites looked at one another. They were terrified. No one had offered to fight the giant before. King Saul sent for David.

'We should not be afraid of this warrior,' David said. 'I will go!'

'You are not even a soldier,' said Saul. 'This giant is a professional fighter.'

'I look after my father's sheep day by day and protect them against lions and bears. God looks after me then; God will save me now.'

Saul gave David his own armour but it was too big and heavy. David chose five small stones from the stream and took aim with his shepherd's sling.

When Goliath saw him, he laughed! But David shouted across the stream.

'You may have a sword, spear and javelin, but I have God himself on my side! Everyone will know today that there is a God is Israel who can save us.'

David whirled the sling around his head. The stone hit Goliath's forehead and the big man fell to the ground. The Philistines ran for their lives!

God's gift to Solomon

'Please make me wise and teach me the difference between right and wrong. Then I will know how to rule your people.'

1 KINGS 3:9

David became king after Saul, and when David died, his son, Solomon, became king.

One night, God spoke to Solomon in a dream.

'Ask for anything that you want,' God said, 'and it will be yours.'

Solomon answered him, 'You have already given me so much! The only thing I need is wisdom, so that I can rule fairly and be a good king.'

God was pleased with Solomon. He gave him the gift of wisdom, but he also gave him wealth and power. And God promised to give him a long life if he continued to obey him and keep his commandments.

One day, two women were brought into Solomon's court with

a complaint against each other.

'Your majesty,' cried one woman, 'this woman and I live in the same house. I gave birth to a son, then, three days later, she also had a son. We both went to sleep with our babies in our arms, but this woman rolled on her baby and he died. So she swapped her dead baby for my living son.'

'You are a liar!' shouted the other woman. 'My son is alive; yours is dead!'

'Bring me a sword!' ordered Solomon. 'Cut the baby in half so that each woman can have a share!' But Solomon knew that the real mother would not let her child suffer in this way.

'Don't harm him!' the first woman pleaded with the king. 'She can have the baby.'

'No, cut him in half!' replied the other woman.

'Give the first woman her baby,' Solomon ordered. 'She is his mother.'

Then everyone in Israel knew that God had given him wisdom to judge between them fairly.

ELIJAH BRINGS BAD NEWS

Ravens brought him bread and meat twice a day,
and he drank water from the brook.

1 KINGS 17:6

Solomon brought peace to Israel. Then he built a beautiful temple for God, made from the best cedar trees in Lebanon and lined with gold-covered wood. Solomon worshipped God in the temple and asked him to bless his people and show them love and compassion.

God promised that he would always be their God and hear his people when they prayed. But he also gave Solomon a warning.

'If you ignore the commandments I have given you, this temple will become a ruin. The people who pass by will know that it is because you did not love the God who brought you out of Egypt and saved you.'

After Solomon's death, the kings of Israel came and went. The kingdom was divided into north and south. One by one, the kings broke God's commandments. Each king was worse than the one before. None of them loved God as King David had, and when Ahab became king, he married Jezebel, who worshipped the Canaanite rain god, Baal. The people who had once worshipped God as the creator of all the world now bowed down to idols they had made with their own hands.

God sent his prophet, Elijah, to King Ahab to warn him to change his ways.

'God—the one true God—has sent me to tell you that there will be no rain. There will be a terrible drought not just for weeks or months, but for years. There will be no rain until God chooses to send it again.'

King Ahab shook with rage. Elijah fled!

God sent Elijah to the eastern side of the River Jordan, where the Cherith Brook would give him clean water to drink in the drought. Ravens brought food for Elijah to eat. Elijah made himself a shelter and stayed there, safe from King Ahab, for a while. God made sure Elijah had everything that he needed.

There was no rain. Day after day, the hot sun beat down and the dawn brought no dew. The ground was dry and parched and soon, even the water in the brook dried up.

The oil that didn't run out

'The Lord God of Israel has promised that your jar of flour won't run out and your bottle of oil won't dry up before he sends rain for the crops.'

1 KINGS 17:14

Elijah trusted God to take care of him. So he was not too surprised when he saw a woman gathering wood in Zarephath.

'Please,I am thirsty. Will you give me some water, and something to eat?' Elijah asked her.

'I have no bread to give you,' she replied. 'I have only enough flour and oil to make one last meal for myself and my son. I am gathering these few sticks to make the fire on which to cook it. Then we will eat it and die, because this is all we have left.'

'Trust God,' said Elijah. 'Bake the bread and share a little with me. God will bless you so that your flour and oil will not run out until God sends rain to the earth again.'

The woman listened to Elijah and trusted God. She baked the bread, and she and her son ate the simple meal with Elijah. When she looked again in the jar, there was enough flour to bake bread for another meal. Again the woman used the flour and oil so they could share their last meal together—and again there was just enough left for another meal. God made sure that Elijah, the woman and her son always had enough to eat during the drought.

After some time had passed, the woman's son became ill and died.

'What have I done to deserve this—to gain my life only to lose my only son?'

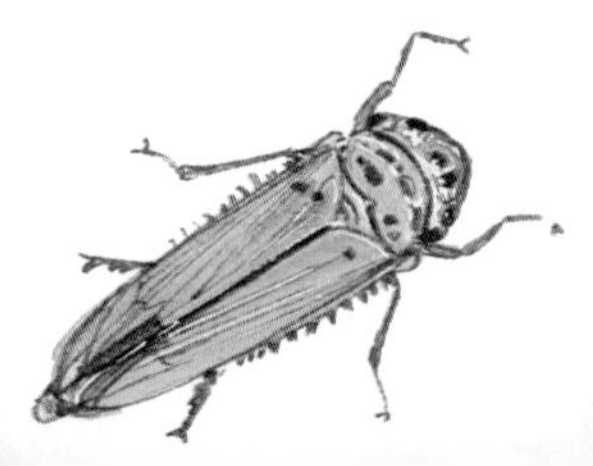

The woman was angry in her grief. Elijah was also very sad at the boy's death. He carried the boy to his room and put him gently on the bed. Then Elijah prayed.

'Lord God,' he cried, 'why have you let this poor boy die? Why have you caused such unhappiness to his mother who has shared her home and food with me? Please, Lord, save this boy. Give him back his life and give the mother back her son!'

God heard Elijah's prayer. The boy breathed again.

'Look! Here is your son—he is alive!' Elijah said.

The woman smiled at Elijah through her tears.

'Now I know that what you say comes from the living God,' she said.

THE CONTEST ON THE MOUNTAIN

'How much longer will you try to have things both ways? If the Lord is God, worship him! But if Baal is God, worship him!'

1 KINGS 18:21

Nearly three years passed, and still, God did not send rain. Then one day God sent Elijah back to King Ahab.

'You are a troublemaker!' Ahab shouted at him.

'No, you are the one who has brought trouble to this land,' said Elijah. 'You were the one who stopped worshipping God! Now let's settle this matter. Call everyone here to Mount Carmel, including all those false prophets.'

So King Ahab and all the people gathered with the 450 prophets of Baal on Mount Carmel, and Elijah spoke to them.

'Today you must choose whom you will serve. If you believe the living God is the real God, then choose him and follow him! If Baal is God, then serve and follow him. Make up your minds and do what is right.

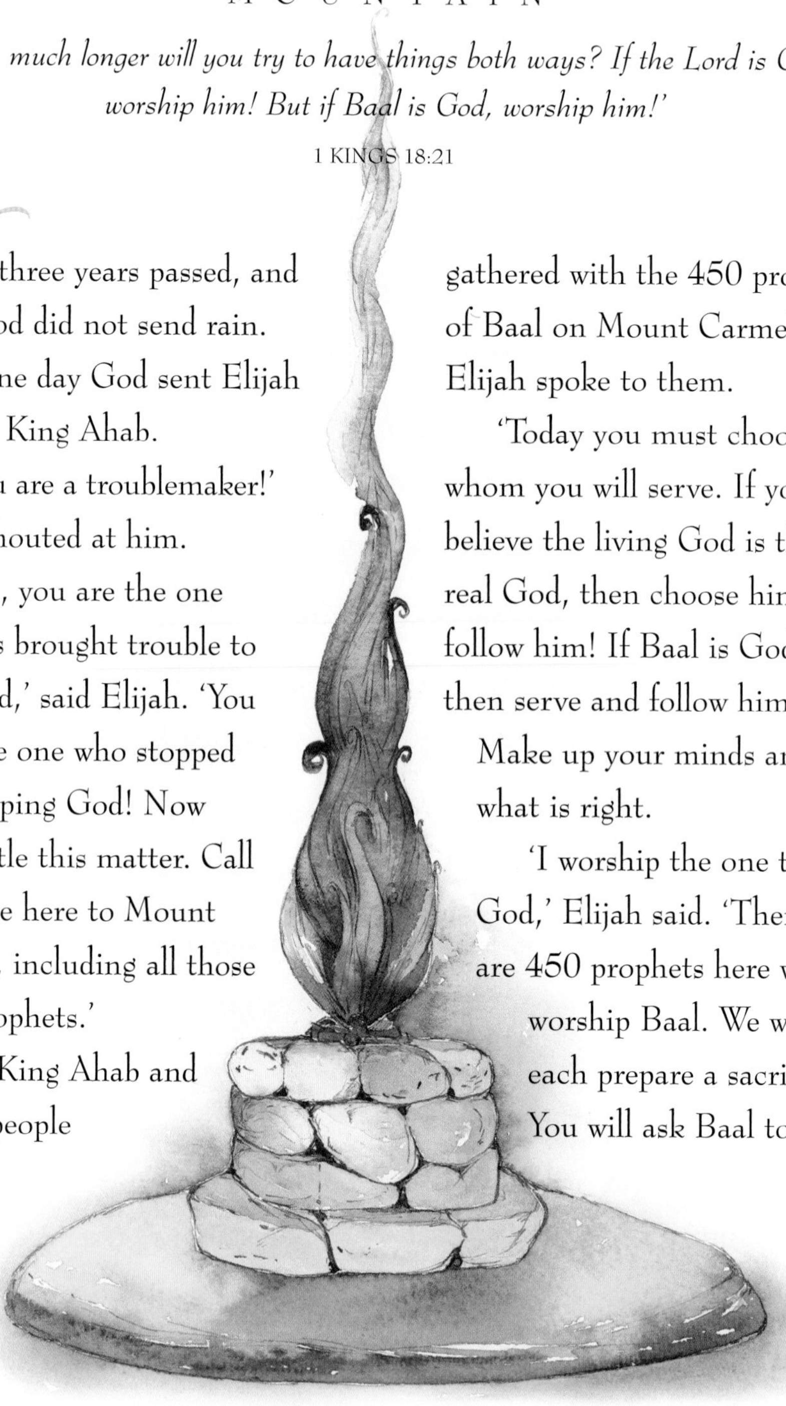

'I worship the one true God,' Elijah said. 'There are 450 prophets here who worship Baal. We will each prepare a sacrifice. You will ask Baal to send down fire to burn it up; I will ask the living God to do the same. Then we will see who really is the one true God.'

The prophets prepared their bull for the sacrifice, and all day they prayed to Baal to send down fire. Nothing happened.

'Is your god asleep?' Elijah taunted them. 'Is he away on holiday and can't answer you?'

The prophets prayed and shouted, but still there was no answer. There was no fire on the altar they had prepared.

Then Elijah made an altar using twelve large stones, to remind the people that they were God's people, the twelve tribes of Israel. He dug a trench around the altar, prepared his sacrifice and finally poured water all over the wood and the sacrifice so that it ran down into the trench. Elijah's sacrifice was soaking wet; it would not burn easily.

Elijah stood in front of everyone and prayed.

'Let the people know now, Lord, that you are the living God who can send down fire on this altar. Let them believe and worship you!'

God answered Elijah and sent down fire. The fire burned up the bull, the stones and the water filling the trench. The people were amazed and believed. They fell on their knees and cried out, 'The Lord is God! The Lord—he is God!'

Then Elijah saw the black clouds form in the sky and God sent rain once more upon the land.

Naaman is healed

'Now I know that the God of Israel is the only God in the whole world.'

2 KINGS 5:15

Elijah remained God's prophet until he was old. Then God took him to heaven in a whirlwind; in a chariot of fire. His friend Elisha served God after him, and God gave to Elisha the faith and power that Elijah had had.

One day, a brave soldier from Samaria came to Elisha for help.

Naaman was an army commander and had in his home a servant girl who had been taken captive on one of the raids on nearby Israelite villages.

The girl liked her master and she loved God. When the girl saw that Naaman's skin was covered in the deadly white patches of leprosy, she urged her mistress to send him to Samaria where Elisha lived. She knew that God had the power to heal Naaman and that Elisha would help him.

First Naaman went to the king of Aram for a letter to take with him for the Israelite king. He also took gifts of silver and gold. But King Joram of Israel was afraid when he received the letter. How could he heal Naaman of his leprosy? He didn't think of Elisha or that God himself could help him. But Elisha heard about the letter.

'Send the man to me,' Elisha said. 'Then he will know that there is a prophet in Israel who loves God.'

So it was that Naaman's horses and chariots were outside the place where Elisha lived. But Elisha did not come outside to greet him. Instead, he sent out a servant with a message.

'Elisha, the prophet, says you must go and wash in the River Jordan seven times. Then you will be healed.'

Naaman was not only surprised, he was angry. Surely the prophet was making fun of him?

'There are better rivers in Damascus where I could wash!' he said. 'Have I come all this way to be told this?'

'But Sir,' said one of his servants, 'if the prophet had told you to do something difficult, you would surely have done it. Don't be too proud to do this simple thing.'

Naaman sighed. But he went down to the River Jordan and he washed. When he came out of the river for the seventh time, his skin was clean and new and the marks of leprosy had gone.

'Now I know that the God of Israel is the only God in the whole world,' he said.

Jonah runs away

The Lord sent a big fish to swallow Jonah, and Jonah was inside the fish for three days and three nights.

JONAH 1:17

The Assyrians were cruel and greedy and threatened God's people. God told Jonah to go to Nineveh, a great city there, and warn them to stop doing wicked things, or they would be destroyed.

Jonah did not want to go. What had Israel's God to do with the Assyrians? So he went to the port of Joppa and paid his fare for Tarshish, about as far in the other direction as he could go. Jonah boarded the ship and went below deck where he fell into a deep sleep.

Once the ship was out to sea, a violent storm arose. It lurched so dangerously in the choppy waves that the sailors on board were sure they would drown. They all prayed to their gods to save them, and threw their cargo over the side to lighten the ship. When the captain realised that Jonah was missing, he went to find him.

'Wake up!' he shouted above the storm. 'Get up and pray to your God!'

Jonah knew that the storm was his fault.

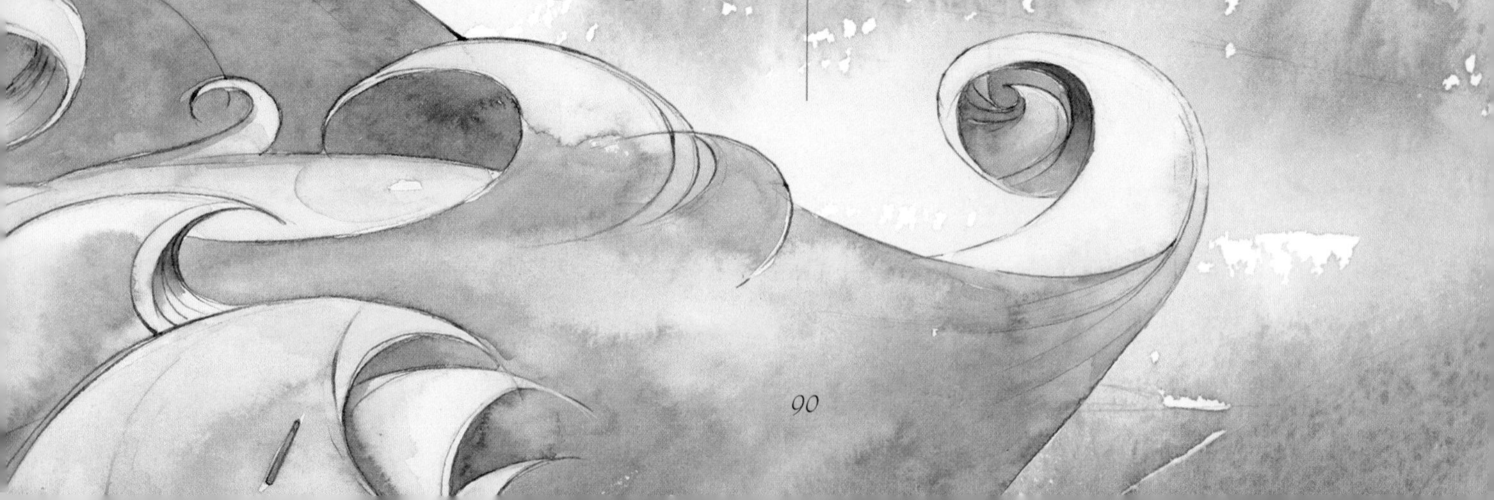

'I worship the God who made the land and the sea,' Jonah replied. 'But I have disobeyed him. If you want to be safe, you must throw me overboard.'

The sailors did not want to kill Jonah, but neither did they want to die. They threw Jonah into the sea. Then the wind dropped and the waves grew calm. The sailors saw the power of the living God.

Jonah fell, deep down in the water. He called to God to help him, and God answered by sending a huge fish to swallow him whole. Jonah stayed inside the body of the fish for three days and three nights. He remembered that he had promised to obey God; he was sorry that he had run away. Only his God had the power to save, and Jonah promised to serve him again.

Then God made the huge fish spit Jonah out on to dry land. This time when God said, 'Go to Nineveh,' Jonah went. Jonah warned the people that they must ask for God's forgiveness and change their ways—or their land would be destroyed in 40 days.

The Assyrians heard what Jonah said and they listened. They asked God to forgive them and began to change the violent way they lived. God heard their prayers, and because God was compassionate, he forgave them.

THE BLAZING, FIERY FURNACE

'The God we worship can save us from you and your flaming furnace.'

DANIEL 3:17

God sent prophets to tell his people how to live. He warned them to listen to him but time after time, they ignored the warnings. They were captured by their enemies. Many were killed. Others were taken away to live in Babylon.

King Nebuchadnezzar saw that there were some talented young men among the captives. He decided to have them trained to work in his palace. Daniel, Shadrach, Meshach and Abednego were among them.

The four friends tried to follow God's commandments even in a strange land. God blessed them so that when they were presented to King Nebuchadnezzar, he was amazed at their wisdom and understanding.

One night, the king had a strange dream. He was so troubled that he demanded not only that his advisers explained to him the meaning of the dream but that they told him what he had dreamed! If they could not, they would all be executed.

Daniel urged his friends to pray and, during the night, God gave Daniel a vision of what the king had dreamed. King Nebuchadnezzar was amazed. He made Daniel ruler over Babylon, and Daniel gave important jobs to his three friends.

Some time later, King Nebuchadnezzar made a statue

of gold so tall and wide that it could be seen for miles around. He commanded everyone to worship the statue or be thrown into a blazing fiery furnace! Everyone fell down to worship the statue, except Daniel's friends, Shadrach, Meshach and Abednego.

'Worship the statue or you will be thrown into the furnace. Then no god can save you!' the king said to them.

'King Nebuchadnezzar,' the friends replied, 'our God is able to save us from the fiery furnace, but even if he does not, we will not worship your statue. We worship God alone.'

The king watched as the three men were tied up and thrown into the fire. Then he stared, amazed at what he saw. Four men were walking around in the fire!

'Get them out!' shouted the king.

Shadrach, Meshach and Abednego stepped out of the furnace, unharmed. They didn't even smell of smoke!

'Your God sent an angel to rescue you, because you were prepared to die for him. Your God alone has the power to save. Praise him!'

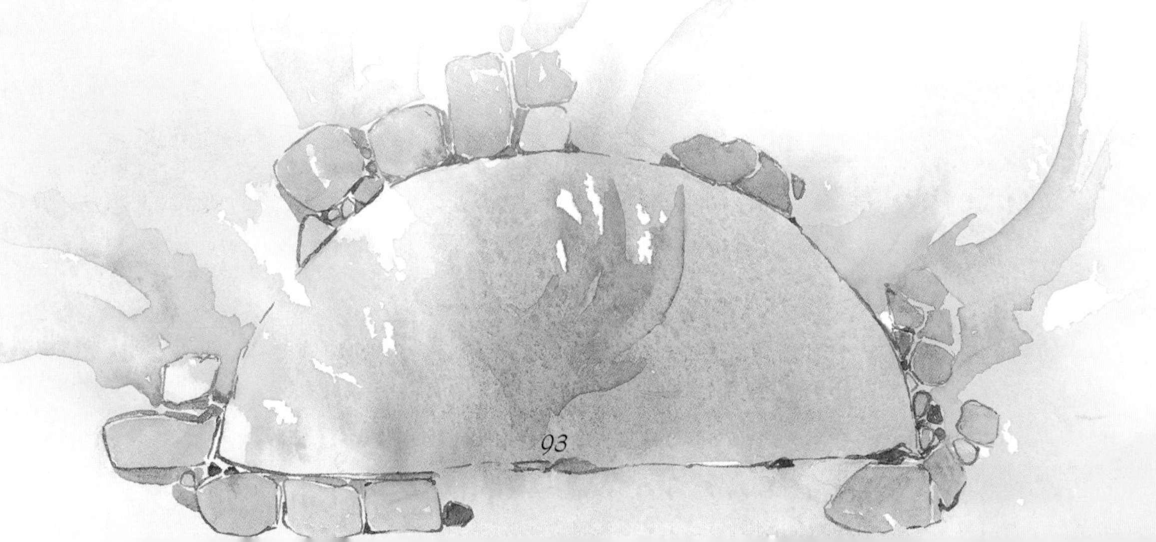

THE PLOT AGAINST DANIEL

'He rescues people and sets them free by working great miracles. Daniel's God has rescued him from the power of the lions.'

DANIEL 6:27

Daniel was a captive in Babylon for many years. When Darius the Mede became King of Babylon, he saw that Daniel was a loyal, hard-working man. He planned to put him in charge of the whole kingdom.

But Daniel had enemies, jealous of his power.

'Your majesty!' they said. 'You are so great that we think you should be honoured. Issue a decree that no one should pray to anyone except you for the next 30 days. And if anyone breaks this decree, throw them to the lions!'

Darius thought for a while. He was flattered. Perhaps it was a good idea. So Darius made the law.

When Daniel heard that the decree had been issued, he went to the place where he prayed three times every day. Daniel knelt down and asked God for help.

Daniel's enemies were watching and waiting. They went straight to the king.

'Your majesty!' they said. 'You said that any person in the land who breaks your law will be thrown to the lions.'

'You know I have,' Darius replied.

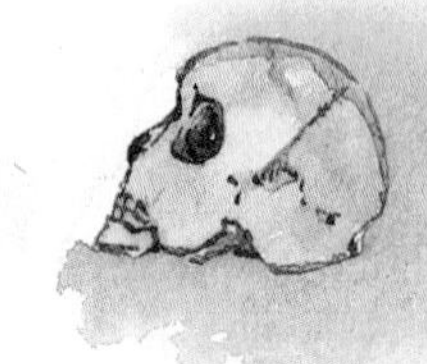

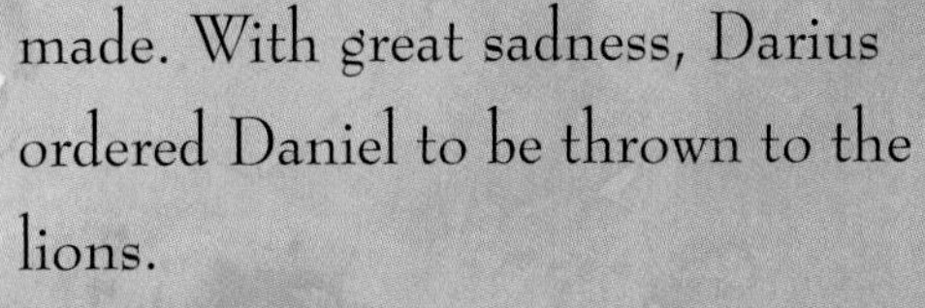

'And this decree cannot be altered,' they persisted.

'It is the law of the Medes and Persians,' he agreed. 'It cannot be altered.'

'Then we are sad to tell you that Daniel ignores the decree. He prays three times a day to his God.'

Immediately Darius realised that the men had tricked him. Now his friend, Daniel, could not be rescued from the law he had made. With great sadness, Darius ordered Daniel to be thrown to the lions.

The next morning, Darius returned to the lions' den.

'Daniel!' he cried. 'Has your God saved you from the teeth of the lions?'

'Yes, your majesty!' Daniel shouted from the den. 'My God sent an angel to close the mouths of the lions. He has saved me!'

'Release Daniel from the den!' cried Darius. 'And punish the evil men who plotted his death.'

Darius issued another decree.

'Everyone in my kingdom must fear and respect Daniel's God. For he is the living God; the God who performs signs and wonders and has the power to save, even from the mouths of lions!'

The Angel in the Temple

'Your wife Elizabeth will have a son, and you must name him John.'

LUKE 1:13

Many years had passed. The Israelites had returned to the land God had given to their ancestors. Herod was now king. But the land was ruled by the Romans, who had made it part of their empire. Roman soldiers walked in the streets and taxes were paid to the Emperor in Rome.

Zechariah, the priest, and his wife Elizabeth lived in the hill country of Judea. They had both loved and served God all their lives, but they had no children, and it was a great sadness for them.

The time came for Zechariah to burn the incense in the temple. The people prayed outside in the sunshine, while inside, where it was cool and quiet, Zechariah was

alone—except that he was not alone. There, on the right hand side of the altar, was an angel.

'Zechariah!' the angel's voice was loud in the stillness of the temple. 'Don't be afraid. God has been listening to your prayers. He will bless you with a son and you will call him John. God's Spirit will guide and help him. He will be a prophet, preparing the people for the future.'

'But... can this really be true?' asked Zechariah. 'It is surely too late for Elizabeth to have a child of her own.'

'I am the angel Gabriel. What I tell you comes straight from God. But because you cannot believe it, you will lose the power to speak until everything I have told you has come true.'

The angel left Zechariah as suddenly as he had appeared.

When Zechariah came out to the people, they knew something strange and wonderful had happened. But Zechariah could not tell them what it was. He could not explain to them about the angel or his message. He could not speak at all.

Some time later, Elizabeth gave birth to a baby boy. Eight days after the birth, when he was circumcised according to the rules God had given his people, they tried to name him Zechariah after his father. But Elizabeth stopped them. She told them he must be called John. When they asked Zechariah, he asked for a writing tablet so he could tell them.

'His name is John,' he wrote.

Then Zechariah could speak again! He praised God who had blessed them with their baby son. All that the angel had promised had come true.

A Saviour Born in Bethlehem

She gave birth to her firstborn son. She dressed him in baby clothes and laid him on a bed of hay, because there was no room for them in the inn.

LUKE 2:7

The angel Gabriel also visited a girl called Mary, who lived in Nazareth in Galilee. Mary was engaged to Joseph, the local carpenter.

'Don't be afraid, Mary,' said Gabriel. 'God is with you! You will bear a son and give him the name Jesus. He will be a king who will reign for ever.'

'But I am not yet married,' said Mary. 'How can I have a baby?'

'The Holy Spirit will make this happen,' said Gabriel. 'Your baby will be the son of God.'

'I will do anything God wants me to,' said Mary.

When Mary found she was expecting a baby, Joseph was anxious about what people would think. She was not yet married. But one night Joseph dreamed that an angel appeared to him.

'Marry Mary and help her care for her baby,' the angel said. 'The Holy Spirit has caused this child to grow inside her. You must call him Jesus. He will be the Saviour of the world.'

So Joseph married Mary.

The Roman emperor, Caesar Augustus, wanted to tax his people. He ordered everyone to go to the town of their ancestors to be counted. Joseph had to take Mary with him to Bethlehem, because he belonged to the family of King

David. But the time had come for Mary's baby to be born.

Bethlehem was full of people who had come for the census. It was already difficult to find somewhere to stay. When Mary gave birth to her baby boy, she wrapped him up and made a bed for him in a manger, because there was no room in the inn.

The same night, shepherds were on the hills outside Bethlehem, looking after their flocks of sheep. Suddenly the dark sky was filled with light as an angel appeared.

'Don't be afraid!' said the angel. 'I have come with good news! Tonight, in Bethlehem, a baby has been born who is the Saviour of the world. You will find him wrapped in strips of cloth, lying in a manger.'

Then they heard the sound of hundreds of angels praising God.

'Praise God in heaven! Peace on earth to everyone who pleases God.'

The shepherds ran down the hillside to look for the baby who had been born that night. They found him, lying in the manger, just as the angels had said, and they told Mary and Joseph about what they had seen and heard.

Wise men from the East

'Where is the child born to be king of the Jews? We saw his star in the east and have come to worship him.'

MATTHEW 2:2

When Jesus was born, wise men in the east saw a new star in the sky.

They decided to set out on a journey, carrying with them gifts, and following the star. They believed a baby king had been born and wanted to worship him.

The men stopped at King Herod's palace when they reached Jerusalem.

'Where is the child born to be king of the Jewish people?' they asked. 'We have come to bring him gifts and worship him.'

Herod was secretly disturbed by their arrival. There was room for only one king in the land. He was that king!

Herod asked the priests and teachers of the law where such a child might be born. They told Herod what they knew from the ancient prophecies: the king would be born in Bethlehem.

Herod then talked to the men from the east. He wanted to know when they had first seen the star—so he would know how old the baby king might be. Then he sent them on their way to Bethlehem.

'You will tell me when you find him?' King Herod said. 'Then I may go to worship him too...'

The wise men travelled towards Bethlehem, where the star seemed to stop over a house. When they went inside, they found the little boy with his mother, Mary. They offered him the gifts they had brought—gold, frankincense and myrrh—and worshipped Jesus, the king of the Jewish people, before returning home.

In the night they dreamed. They were warned that it was not safe to return to King Herod, so they went back a different way.

Joseph was also warned by an angel to take Mary and Jesus away to Egypt, where they would be safe from the evil King Herod.

Meanwhile Herod waited. When he realised that the wise men were not coming back, he was very angry. Herod was a cruel king. He gave orders for all the little boys under two years old in the area to be killed so that Jesus must surely be killed with them.

But Jesus was safely in Egypt.

Joseph kept him there until Herod had died. When it was safe to return, an angel told Joseph that they could make their home in Nazareth in Galilee.

JOHN THE BAPTIST

'In the desert someone is shouting, "Get the road ready for the Lord! Make a straight path for him."'

LUKE 3:4

Zechariah's son, John, had grown up to be a man and was living alone in the desert.

God had a special job for him to do, as a prophet, telling the people how he wanted them to live. John looked wild, wearing clothes of camel's hair and eating strange foods. But the people listened to him. They saw that God spoke through him.

'Stop doing things that are wrong and obey God,' John told them. 'Be baptised to show that you are sorry and that God has forgiven you.'

Many people came to the River Jordan and John baptised them.

'Show that you love God by the way you live,' John said to them. 'Give away what you don't need to someone who does. Share your food with people who have nothing. Live honestly and fairly—don't cheat or bully people. I am no one; I am preparing the way for someone much greater. I will baptise you with water, but he will baptise you with God's own Spirit.'

One day Jesus stood on the banks of the River Jordan and listened as John spoke to the people. He had grown up too and had been working as a carpenter for many years. He went to John and asked to be baptised.

'I cannot baptise you! Surely you should baptise me!' John said.

But Jesus persuaded him. As he came out of the water, God's

Spirit came down from heaven like a dove and rested on Jesus. Everyone heard God's voice.

'You are my Son. I love you very much. I am pleased with you.'

Afterwards Jesus spent 40 days in the desert. He had nothing to eat and was very weak and hungry. God's enemy, the devil, came to test him, to see if he would break God's laws. But the devil was defeated. He tried to tempt Jesus, but Jesus would do nothing wrong.

Jesus Begins His Ministry

Jesus said to them, 'Come with me! I will teach you how to bring in people instead of fish.'

MATTHEW 4:19

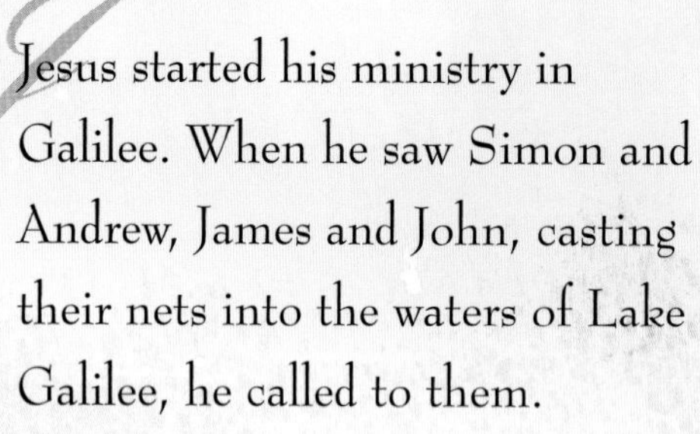

Jesus started his ministry in Galilee. When he saw Simon and Andrew, James and John, casting their nets into the waters of Lake Galilee, he called to them.

'Come and follow me!' Jesus called to them.

They got out of the boat and went with Jesus straight away. The four fishermen were the first of Jesus' twelve disciples. He went to their homes in Capernaum and taught in the synagogue, healing people who were ill.

One day, Jesus and some of his disciples went to a wedding in Cana. When the wine ran out, Mary asked Jesus to help them.

'Do what he asks,' she whispered to the servants.

'Fill these six jars with water,' Jesus said. The jars were used for washing and were huge, each holding many gallons of water.

Then Jesus asked them to pour some out and offer it to the man in charge of the feast. The man tasted it. The servants knew it was water but a miracle had happened. It had become the most wonderful wine.

Soon people began to talk about how Jesus was able to heal people and talk about God's love in a way no one had before. But the real test was in Nazareth, the place where Jesus had grown up, where people knew him.

Jesus went to the synagogue on the

Sabbath day and read the scroll containing the words of the prophet Isaiah.

'God's Spirit is on me,' read Jesus. 'He has chosen me to bring good news to the poor, to free those who are in chains, to give sight to the blind, to help those who are suffering and to tell everyone that God's blessing has come.'

Jesus rolled up the scroll and sat down.

'Isaiah wrote those words hundreds of years ago but today, here, you have seen it come true.'

Amazing things happen

When Jesus saw how much faith they had, he said to the crippled man, 'My friend, your sins are forgiven.'

LUKE 5:20

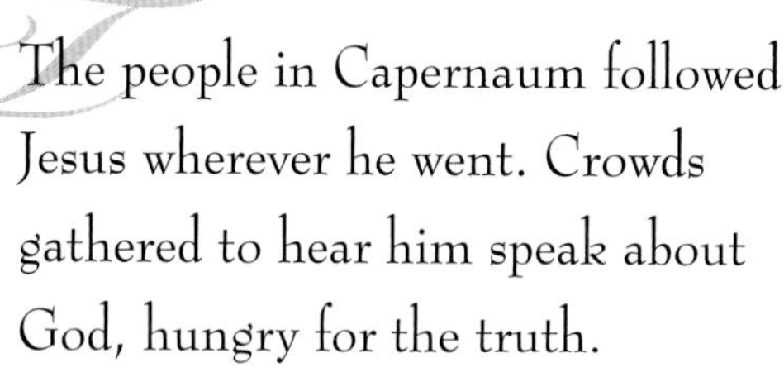

The people in Capernaum followed Jesus wherever he went. Crowds gathered to hear him speak about God, hungry for the truth.

Four men, carrying their friend who couldn't walk, were very keen to find Jesus. But when they reached the house where Jesus was teaching, people were packed all around him, spilling out of the doorway. The men could not get close to him.

Seeing the steps outside the house, leading to the roof, the men climbed up, carrying their friend on a mat. They dug through the roof, sending the mud and bits of twig down on the people below. By the time there was a hole large enough to lower the man down in front of Jesus, amazed faces were looking up at them!

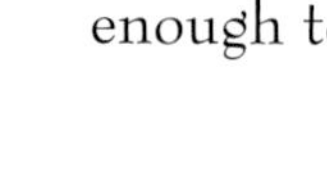

Jesus saw the faith of the four men. He looked at the paralysed man.

'Go,' he said, 'your sins are forgiven.'

The religious teachers around Jesus were shocked. They knew only God could forgive sins! But Jesus knew what they were thinking.

'Which is easier,' Jesus asked, 'to forgive sins or make a paralysed man walk? For God, nothing is impossible.' Then he spoke to the man on the mat again. 'Stand up, take your mat, and go home.'

The man stood up and picked up his mat. His friends

were overjoyed. Everyone else was amazed! They knew they had witnessed a miracle and they praised God.

After this, Jesus asked Matthew to join him. Matthew collected money for the Romans but, just like the fishermen, when Jesus challenged Matthew to follow him, he stopped what he was doing straight away and went along with him.

Matthew invited Jesus back to his house for dinner with many of his friends. But this shocked the religious leaders.

'Why does Jesus mix with such terrible people?' they asked the disciples.

Jesus answered for himself. 'Healthy people don't need a doctor,' he told them. 'I am here because these people need me.'

So it was that Jesus made enemies as well as many friends and followers.

The Sermon on the Mount

'But you must always act like your Father in heaven.'

MATTHEW 5:48

One day Jesus walked up the hillside overlooking the Sea of Galilee. He sat down and began to talk to the people who had followed him there.

'God blesses people who are not proud, but who know how much they need God's help and forgiveness.

'Live according to God's commandments, and you will be like a little salt in the cooking pot, making the whole meal taste good. You will be like a lamp shining brightly in a dark place, bringing light so that everyone can see.

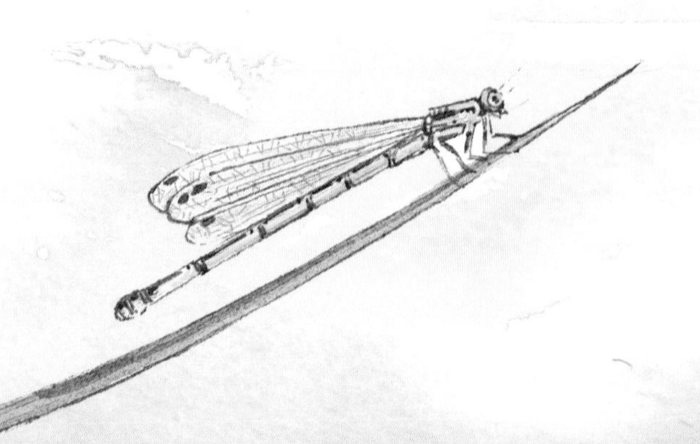

'Don't try to get your own back if someone hurts you. Instead, be kind to them. Go out of your way to help everyone. Love your enemies as well as your friends and family. God is perfect. We must try to be like him.

'Don't pray using empty, meaningless words so that other people will notice you. Be honest with God. God knows what you want to tell him before you begin to speak. Talk to God simply and quietly, saying something like this:

'Our Father in heaven, your name is holy. Bring your kingdom to earth so that kindness and justice may be done here as they are done in heaven. Give us the food we need today. And forgive us all the hurt we have caused you, just as we forgive people who have hurt us. Do not test us beyond our strength, and keep us safe from evil.

'Don't worry about what you will eat or drink, or what clothes you're going to wear. Look around you at the wild birds. They rely on God to feed them. God cares about them, but he cares about you even more. You won't live longer by worrying about anything. As for worrying about clothes, look at the beautiful lilies that grow in the fields. They don't work or dress themselves, but God has made them beautiful.

'Put God first, and he will make sure that you have everything you need—and much more besides.

'Listen to me, and you will be like a wise man who builds his house on a rock. You will have firm foundations so that when the rain batters the house and the wind blows, your house will remain firm and solid.

'If you ignore all I have said you will be like a foolish man who builds his house on sand. You will have no foundations when the wind blows and your house will fall down. Be like the wise man; listen and act on what you hear.'

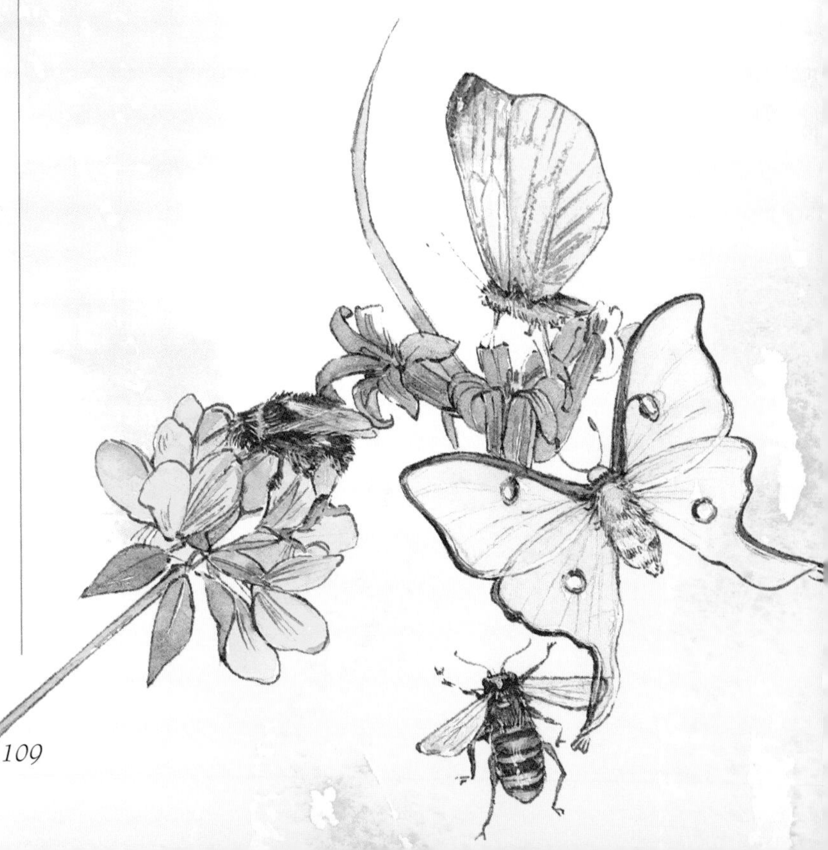

Faith in Jesus

'I am not good enough for you to come into my house. And I am certainly not worthy to come to you. Just say the word, and my servant will get well.'

LUKE 7:6–7

When Jesus returned to Capernaum, a Roman centurion came up to him, agitated and clearly in need of help.

'My servant is very ill. He is in terrible pain and cannot move. Will you help him?'

'Let me come to your house,' said Jesus. 'Then I will heal him.'

But the centurion stopped Jesus.

'Lord, I don't deserve to have you in my house. But I know that if you just say that my servant is healed, he will be healed. I am used to having authority over people. I expect people below me to obey my orders. I know you have the same kind of authority over his illness.'

Jesus was amazed.

'I have not found anyone here with faith like yours,' he said. 'Go home now, and you will find that your servant is better.'

The centurion went home to find that his servant had recovered, just as Jesus had said.

Soon afterwards Jesus and his disciples visited the town of Nain. A large crowd followed even

though it was many miles away. As they approached, they watched a funeral procession making its way to the little cemetery outside the city gates.

Jesus saw the body of a young man on a stretcher and his weeping mother following behind. She was a widow and with her only son now dead, she was quite alone.

Jesus saw the widow's sadness. He went up to the stretcher and touched it.

'Sit up, young man,' Jesus said to the body lying there.

The young man opened his eyes imediately and sat up on the stretcher. He spoke to his astonished mother who could hardly believe the miracle she was witnessing. Then there was much joy and amazement among all the people there.

People could not stop talking about what had happened. The news about Jesus, the prophet who could raise people from the dead, spread all over the country.

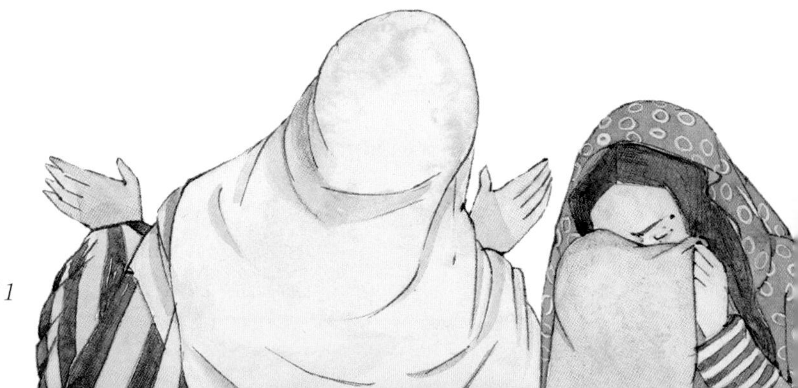

Jesus performs more miracles

The men in the boat were amazed and said, 'Who is this? Even the wind and the waves obey him.'

MATTHEW 8:27

Jesus was tired after teaching the crowds one evening.

'Let's go across to the other side of the lake,' he said to his twelve disciples. Then Jesus lay down in the boat with a cushion under his head and fell asleep.

Suddenly the calm lake became choppy. Water began to crash over the side of the boat as the wind rose. The men clung to the mast. Even the fishermen among them were afraid.

'Master, help us!' they shouted. 'We're all going to die!'

Jesus woke and stood up.

'Be calm!' he said to the wind and waves. The wind dropped as suddenly as it had come up and the sea was still.

'Why were you afraid?' Jesus asked the frightened men. 'Don't you trust me?'

'Who is he?' they asked one another. 'Even the wind and the waves obey him!'

Crowds came out to meet Jesus when they arrived in Capernaum. Jairus, the leader of the synagogue, hurried to speak to Jesus.

'Please help us,' he cried. 'My little girl is dying!'

Jesus went to Jairus' house

straight away, but as they were moving through the crowds, Jesus stopped. He turned to look behind him.

'Who touched me?' he asked.

'Master,' Peter said, 'there are people everywhere. Anyone could have touched you.'

Then a woman stepped forward. 'I touched your cloak,' she said. 'I have been ill for many years. No doctor has been able to help me. I knew that if only I could touch the hem of your cloak, it would be enough.'

'Don't be afraid,' Jesus said. 'Your faith has healed you.'

They were interrupted by someone from Jairus' house.

'It's too late,' he told Jairus. 'Your daughter is dead.'

'Come with me,' Jesus said. 'Your daughter will be healed.'

When he arrived at Jairus' house, Jesus sent the weeping people away. He went inside with the girl's father and mother, and with Peter, James and John.

'Get up, little girl,' Jesus said.

The girl's eyes opened, and she began to breathe again.

'She is hungry,' smiled Jesus. 'Give her something to eat.'

Jairus and his wife were astonished. Their daughter had been dead, but now she was alive.

JESUS CARES FOR THE PEOPLE

When he saw the crowds, he felt sorry for them.

MATTHEW 9:36

One day Jesus was teaching the people and healing those who were ill until it was almost dark. He saw that they were hungry and asked Philip, who lived nearby, if there were somewhere where bread could be bought for them.

'Master, there are over 5000 people! We couldn't afford to buy bread for everyone here.'

Andrew brought a boy to Jesus who had with him a picnic lunch.

'This boy says he will share his five small barley rolls and two little fish,' said Andrew.

Jesus took the food. He thanked God and asked him to bless it. Then he broke it into pieces and gave it to his disciples, who shared the bread and fish among the people. Everyone ate until they had had enough. Then the disciples went among the people and collected twelve baskets full of leftover pieces. It was a miracle.

On another occasion, a group of people brought to Jesus a deaf man who needed his help. Jesus put his fingers in the man's ears, then put some of his own saliva on the man's tongue. Then he prayed for the man, asking for God's help.

Suddenly the deaf man could hear and speak! His friends were so excited, they couldn't stop telling people about what had happened.

In another place Jesus saw ten men who suffered from leprosy standing together, dressed in rags that covered their damaged faces and limbs. Their skin disease had made them outcasts.

'Jesus! Please help us!' they called to him.

'Go to the priest and show him your skin,' Jesus told them. 'You have been healed.'

Suddenly they saw that the leprosy had gone! Their skin was whole again. One of the men, who came from Samaria, ran back to thank Jesus and praise God. Jesus looked into the distance at those who were still walking away.

'I thought there were ten of you,' Jesus said sadly. 'Are you the only one who wanted to thank God?'

Jesus also healed a number of people on the Sabbath day—a man with a withered hand, a man who couldn't walk, a woman who was bent double and couldn't stand up straight—but this made the religious leaders angry, and they plotted against him.

Stories Jesus Told

'... There is more happiness in heaven because of one sinner who turns to God than over ninety-nine good people who don't need to.'

LUKE 15:7

Jesus taught his disciples about God. He taught whole crowds of people who followed him, often by telling stories. Jesus also answered the questions of anyone who really wanted to know the truth about God.

'Teacher,' someone once asked. 'What must I do to have everlasting life?'

'What does God's Law say?' Jesus asked.

'Love God with all your heart, your soul, your mind and your strength. Love your neighbour as you love yourself,' replied the man. 'But who is my neighbour?'

Jesus told a story to answer him about a man who was beaten and robbed on the road from Jerusalem to Jericho. A priest did not stop to help the wounded man. A Levite also walked by without stopping. But a Samaritan stopped and bandaged his wounds, helped him on to his own donkey, and took him to an inn. He paid the innkeeper to look after the man till he was well again.

'Who do you think was a neighbour to the wounded man?'

'The one who helped him,' said the man.

'That's what you must do,' said Jesus.

Jesus also told people about God's love.

'Once there was a rich farmer whose land produced an excellent harvest,' said Jesus. 'He had to build new barns so he could store everything he owned. He ate and drank all he wanted, sure that this would make him happy. But God said to him, "This is the last night left to you on earth. You have stored up many things, but

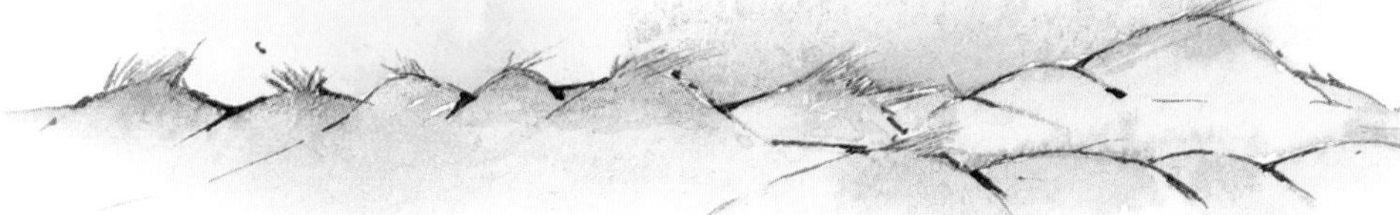

now you must die and leave them all behind." The rich man's wealth was now no good to him at all. So, live for other people, thinking of their needs before your own. God will look after you, and you will store treasure in heaven, where no moth can eat it and no thief can steal it.'

'If you owned 100 sheep, and one of them was lost,' said Jesus, 'you'd make sure the others were safe and go looking for it. You wouldn't rest till that one lost sheep was found. God is just the same. He cares about everyone and will not be happy until he has saved the one who has wandered off the right path.'

Jesus told people about the way God wanted them to live.

Mary, Martha and Lazarus

Jesus then said, 'I am the one who raises the dead to life! Everyone who has faith in me will live, even if they die.'

JOHN 11:25

Jesus had friends in the village of Bethany just outside Jerusalem. Lazarus and his sisters, Mary and Martha, made Jesus welcome whenever he passed through.

On one visit, Martha had busied herself preparing food to make sure everything was just right for her visitors. But when she saw that her sister, Mary, sat listening to Jesus while she worked, Martha was unhappy.

'Lord,' she said to Jesus, 'tell Mary to come and help me. Surely it is not right that she does nothing while I am working hard?'

'There is always work to do, Martha,' Jesus answered. 'Sometimes it's good to spend time with people instead.'

Some time later, Jesus heard that their brother, Lazarus, was seriously ill. Mary and Martha sent a message, asking Jesus to come and help him. But Jesus did not go immediately. He knew that they would see an even greater miracle if he stayed away.

Martha went to meet Jesus when he arrived in Bethany. Lazarus had already died and been buried for four days. There were many friends

there, weeping with the sisters.

'If you had been here when my brother was ill, I know he would still be alive!' she told him. 'But it is not too late even now. God will give you what you ask for.'

'You are right, Martha. Lazarus will rise from the dead,' said Jesus.

'I know that at the end of time he will rise again,' she answered.

Jesus replied, 'I am the one who raises the dead to life! Everyone who has faith in me will live, even if they die. Do you believe this, Martha?'

'Yes, I do!' said Martha. 'I believe that you are the chosen one, the Son of God himself!' and she ran to fetch her sister.

Mary came with all Lazarus' friends and together they went to her brother's tomb. Then Jesus cried too. He asked them to open the tomb.

'But Lazarus has been dead for days!' cried Martha.

'You trust me, don't you, Martha?' said Jesus. Jesus then called to Lazarus.

The man walked out of the tomb still wearing his grave clothes. It was a miracle.

Mary and Martha were overjoyed! Many of their friends, who had seen what had happened, put their trust in Jesus.

Changed lives

'The Son of Man came to look for and to save people who are lost.'

LUKE 19:10

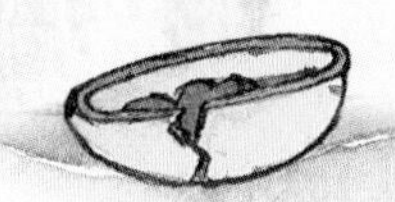

People followed Jesus wherever he went. So although Bartimaeus was blind, he knew that something unusual was happening. He could hear it!

'Who is it?' he shouted out. 'What's happening?'

'It's Jesus,' someone answered him. 'The teacher from Nazareth is here in Jericho!'

Bartimaeus had heard everything people had been saying about Jesus. He didn't need eyes to know that Jesus had healed a paralysed man so he could walk and a deaf man so he could hear.

'Help me!' he shouted out. 'Jesus, over here!'

'Sshh! Jesus is busy!' someone said.

'Jesus! Help me!' Bartimaeus shouted even louder.

'Bring that man to me,' Jesus said.

Bartimaeus struggled

to his feet and felt his way through the crowd until he was standing in front of Jesus.

'What do you want me to do for you?' asked Jesus.

'I want to see,' replied Bartimaeus.

'Your faith has healed you,' replied Jesus.

Bartimaeus opened his eyes—and he could see! He joined all the people following Jesus.

The crowd was even thicker further along the road. Zacchaeus, the tax collector, could not see over their heads, yet he wanted to see Jesus too. He found a tree with low branches and climbed up to get a better view.

But when Jesus reached the tree, he stopped and looked up.

'Come down, Zacchaeus!' said Jesus. 'I was hoping to come to your house today.'

Zacchaeus almost fell out of the tree. Jesus! Knowing his name, coming to his house! But the people in the crowd muttered among themselves. Why would Jesus want to be with a man who cheated and stole from them; a man who worked for the Romans?

Zacchaeus saw their faces and heard what they were saying.

'Jesus!' he said. 'I want to put things right. I want to give half of everything I own to the poor. And I will pay back four times the amount I owe if anyone feels I have cheated them.'

'This man understands why I have come,' Jesus said. 'I am here to find people who have forgotten how to follow God's ways—and save them!'

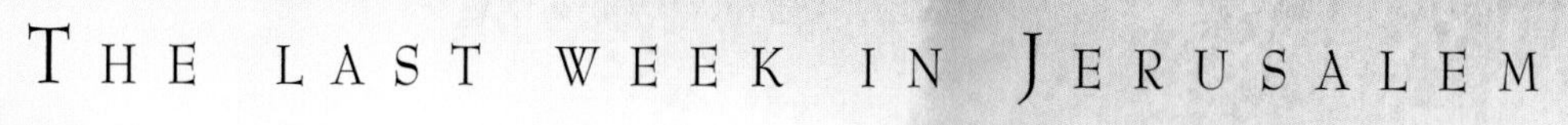

The last week in Jerusalem

'Blessed is the king who comes in the name of the Lord!
Peace in heaven and glory to God.'

LUKE 21:30

It was time for Jesus and his friends to go with many others into Jerusalem to celebrate the Passover festival.

Jesus asked two of his disciples to go on ahead and bring back for him a young donkey so that he could ride it into the town. Everything had been prepared. The men found the donkey and brought it to Jesus. They covered its back with a cloak and Jesus sat on it and rode towards the city gates from the Mount of Olives. It was a prophecy come true.

There were crowds of people going into the town but soon they parted to greet Jesus. Some spread cloaks on the ground for the donkey to walk on. Others cut huge palm branches from the trees and spread them over the road. The path was lined with people waving and cheering.

'Hosanna!' they cried. 'Praise to the king who comes to save us!'

Some of the people in Jerusalem turned to see who this important person could be.

'It's Jesus!' they were told. 'He's a prophet from Nazareth.'

Jesus and his disciples made their way to the temple courts but as soon as Jesus got there, he was shocked at what he saw. The money changers and people selling doves were not only trading but cheating the people who had come there to worship God.

Jesus drove them out,

overturning their tables so that money scattered everywhere.

'This is God's house,' Jesus said, 'but you have made it a place of thieves and robbers!'

The chief priests and the Pharisees watched Jesus. They saw what he did to the money changers. They listened as Jesus taught the people about God every day. They heard as children gathered around him singing his praises. They watched as he healed the blind and people who could not walk. The chief priests and elders were his enemies. They plotted to get rid of Jesus but because the people loved him, they realised that they could no nothing without causing a riot.

One day Jesus watched some rich men putting money into the temple treasury boxes. Then a poor widow slipped two small coins into the box too.

'That woman has given far more than anyone else,' Jesus said. 'The people who gave large gifts still had plenty left—they hardly noticed what they had given. But she gave everything she had to God.'

THE PLOT TO KILL JESUS

Judas Iscariot… went to the chief priests and asked, 'How much will you give me if I help you arrest Jesus?'

MATTHEW 26:14–15

Jesus had dinner with his friend Lazarus a few days before Passover. He sat with his disciples around the table while Martha served them food.

Mary then shocked everyone in the room. She prepared to wash Jesus' feet—but instead of using water, she poured out some expensive perfume from a jar so that the whole room was filled with the beautiful scent. Then Mary wiped Jesus' feet, not with a towel, but with her long dark hair.

People shook their heads disapprovingly.

'What a waste of some expensive perfume!' Judas Iscariot said. 'We could have sold it and given the money to the poor!'

Judas looked after the money people gave to help Jesus with his work. But Jesus knew that Judas sometimes took money from the purse to spend on himself.

'Leave Mary alone,' Jesus answered. 'She has shown me her love in doing this and prepared me for my burial. The poor will always need your help, but I will not be here much longer.'

Judas was secretly very angry.

He knew he couldn't stay with Jesus any more. Instead he started to think of ways to betray him to his enemies.

The chief priests were also plotting among themselves behind closed doors.

'We can't let Jesus carry on teaching the people for much longer,' they said. 'We must find a way to destroy him.'

'But the people love him,' said one. 'Jerusalem is too busy with all the people who have come for the Passover. There will be a riot if we have Jesus arrested when so many of his supporters are here.'

Then their opportunity came. Judas Iscariot came to find them.

'What will you give me if I betray Jesus?' he asked.

'Thirty silver coins,' came their answer. The coins were counted out and put on the table in front of him. Judas looked at the money. Then he picked it up quickly and put it away. Now all Judas had to do was wait for a quiet moment when Jesus would be alone.

The chief priests smiled at each other. One of the twelve, one of Jesus' closest friends and disciples, was now on their side. Judas could betray Jesus when he was not surrounded by crowds of people. Perhaps their problems would soon be ended.

The Servant King

'But I am giving you a new command. You must love each other, just as I have loved you.;

JOHN 13:34

It was almost time for the Passover feast.

Jesus sent Peter and John to make arrangements for them to celebrate in an upper room in Jerusalem. They met the night before to have supper together.

Jesus took a towel, filled a basin with water and washed the feet of each of his disciples. Peter objected. Why was Jesus doing the job of a servant?

'I have done this to show you how you should treat each other,' said Jesus. 'Follow my example. Take care of each other and people will know that you are my followers.'

When they sat down to eat, Jesus told them that one of them would betray him. And during the meal, Judas slipped out of the room to go to the chief priests.

Jesus held the loaf of unleavened bread and thanked God for it. He broke it into pieces and shared it with his friends around the table.

'Take this and eat it. This is my body, which is given up for you,' he said. 'Remember me whenever you eat bread together.' Then Jesus picked up a cup of red wine. 'Take and drink this. This wine is my blood, shed for you so that your sins may be forgiven.'

Jesus' friends looked at one another. They did not understand what Jesus was telling them. They still did not understand that he was soon to die and that afterwards God would raise him from death.

'You cannot follow me where I am going,' said Jesus.

'I will never leave you,' said Peter, 'even if the others do!'

'Peter,' Jesus replied sadly, 'before the cock crows tomorrow morning, you will have denied three times that you even know me.

'Don't be afraid,' said Jesus. 'Trust God. I am going to prepare a place for you and there is plenty of room for everyone there.'

'How can we follow you if we don't know the way,' asked Thomas.

'I am the way,' answered Jesus. 'I am the truth and the life. Come to God through me. If you know me, then you know God too, and later I will give you the Holy Spirit, who will remind you of all I have taught you, and help you to obey me and live the way God wants you to.'

Jesus prays in the garden

'Father, you can do anything. Don't make me suffer by having me drink from this cup. But do what you want, and not what I want.'

MARK 14:36

There was an olive grove outside Jerusalem called the Garden of Gethsemane. Jesus went to pray there after supper. He asked Peter, James and John to walk a little way with him.

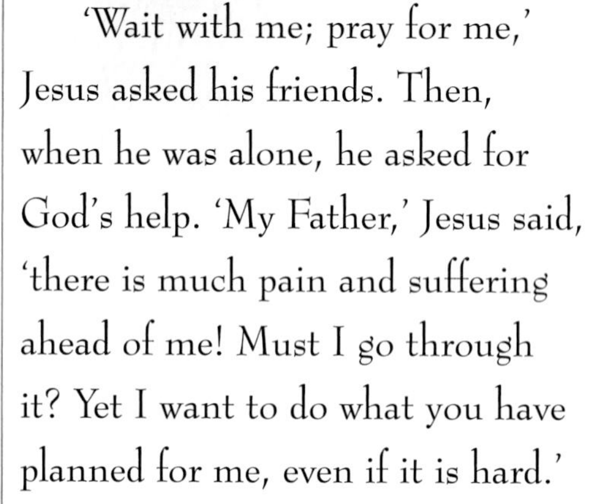

'Wait with me; pray for me,' Jesus asked his friends. Then, when he was alone, he asked for God's help. 'My Father,' Jesus said, 'there is much pain and suffering ahead of me! Must I go through it? Yet I want to do what you have planned for me, even if it is hard.'

Jesus stood up and walked back to his friends, but all of them were asleep.

'Couldn't you stay awake even for an hour?' he said. 'Do you have so little strength?'

Then Jesus went again to pray.

'Father, if this is what you want, then I am ready to obey you.'

Again he went back to his disciples. They could not keep their eyes open.

But now it was too late. Through the trees people were approaching, a noisy crowd, some with clubs or swords in their hands. Jesus' friends recognised the man in front of them. It was Judas Iscariot.

Judas went up to Jesus, and greeted him with a kiss. It was a sign of friendship, but with it, Judas betrayed his friend.

The disciples looked on, horrified, as the men began to march Jesus away as if he were a criminal. His friends ran away, frightened for their lives.

Peter followed at a safe distance in the darkness, afraid to draw attention to himself but desperate to see what would happen to Jesus. Peter watched as Jesus was taken to the house of Caiaphas, the High Priest, and joined some people around a fire in the courtyard. Suddenly a servant girl pointed at Peter.

'Aren't you one of Jesus' friends?' she asked.

'No,' said Peter, getting to his feet. 'I don't know the man!'

A little later another servant spoke to him.

'You went around with Jesus!' she said.

'Not me!' Peter was angry. 'I'm not his friend.'

It was almost dawn when someone else accused Peter.

'You must know Jesus! You have a Galilean accent!'

'I don't know what you're talking about!' Peter answered.

At that moment, a cock crowed as Jesus looked out at Peter. It was dawn, and Peter remembered what Jesus had said would happen. Peter had denied his friend three times before dawn.

A Crown of Thorns

Pilate asked them, 'What am I to do with Jesus, who is called the Messiah?' They all yelled, 'Nail him to a cross!'

MATTHEW 27:22

Pontius Pilate was the Roman governor. He did not want trouble. He did not want to upset the Jewish priests. But he had questioned the man, Jesus of Nazareth, and could find nothing under Roman law that would justify punishment by death.

Pilate decided to ask the crowd outside, who were waiting for his verdict on the man in front of him.

'It is your custom at Passover to release a prisoner,' he said. 'Shall I release Barabbas, the murderer, or Jesus, whom some say is your Messiah, your king?'

There were people in the crowd who were friends of Jesus, some whom he had healed. But there were also complete strangers and people put there by the chief priests and elders to make sure that Jesus was not set free.

'We want Barabbas!' they shouted. 'Set Barabbas free!'

'Then what shall I do with Jesus?' asked Pilate.

'Nail him to a cross!' came the answer from the crowd. 'Nail him to a cross!'

Pilate looked at the angry faces below him and shook his head. He asked for water to wash his hands.

'I am not guilty of this man's death,' he said.

Pilate had Barabbas released, but Jesus was marched away by the soldiers.

They took away Jesus' clothes and put on him the cloak of a Roman soldier. They put a stick in his right hand and made a crown for him of sharp thorns twisted together. When they forced it down on his head, blood trickled down his face. Then the soldiers mocked him, calling him 'King of the Jews!', and spat in his face. Finally, they beat him again and again.

Jesus was exhausted. Cut and bruised from the beating, he was forced to bear the weight of the wooden bar and carry it along the streets to the place where he would be crucified. Jesus stumbled and fell down.

The streets were lined with people, some weeping, others jeering.

'Hey! You!' said a soldier to a man in the crowd. 'Carry this!'

Jesus walked ahead as the man, Simon from Cyrene, carried the long piece of wood on his shoulder till they reached the place of crucifixion outside the city walls.

JESUS DIES ON THE CROSS

Jesus said, 'Father, forgive these people! They don't know what they're doing.'

LUKE 23:34

The soldiers led Jesus away to Golgotha, the Place of the Skull.

Two other men were led out to be crucified that day, both of them thieves. Jesus was nailed to the wooden bar and hoisted up between them.

'Forgive them, Father!' said Jesus. 'They don't know what they are doing!'

The crowds watched and waited while the soldiers jeered.

'You saved other people, but you can't help yourself!' they said.

One of the thieves, who hung beside Jesus, shouted to him.

'If you really are God's Son, then save us all!'

'Be quiet!' said the other thief. 'We deserve our punishment. This man has done nothing wrong.' Then he spoke to Jesus. 'Remember me,' he said.

'Today you will be with me in paradise,' Jesus replied.

John, one of Jesus' disciples, was standing near the foot of the cross. A group of women, including Jesus' own mother, was also there.

'Treat this man as your son,' Jesus called to his mother. Then to his friend John, he said, 'Treat this woman as if she were your own mother.'

At midday the sky turned black. At around three o'clock in the afternoon, Jesus called out loud, 'It is finished!' and breathed his last breath.

Joseph of Arimathea was a member of the Jewish Council, the Sanhedrin. He and Nicodemus were secret followers of Jesus, and neither man had been among those who plotted to kill him. As it was almost the Sabbath, Joseph went to Pontius Pilate and asked if Jesus' body could be taken down from the cross and buried. Then, with Pilate's permission, Joseph went with Nicodemus and took Jesus' broken body from the cross. There were wounds in his hands and feet, and in his side where a soldier had stabbed him with a sword to check that he was dead.

The two men wrapped Jesus in strips of linen with myrrh and aloes, and placed his body in the newly-made tomb that Joseph had

prepared for his own burial. Then they rolled a great stone across the entrance to seal it.

Mary Magdalene and her friend watched where they put Jesus' body.

JESUS IS ALIVE!

'The people who have faith in me without seeing me are the ones who are really blessed!'

JOHN 20:29

Early on Sunday morning, Mary Magdalene went to anoint Jesus' body with spices. She was amazed to find that the stone had been rolled away and the tomb was empty. Then Mary saw a man in the garden. As soon as he spoke her name, she knew that it was Jesus!

'Go and tell the others what you have seen,' Jesus said gently.

Later, two of Jesus' followers walked along the road to Emmaus with a stranger. When he ate supper with them, they realised that he was Jesus, risen from the dead! By the time they had returned to tell the others, they found that Peter had also seen Jesus alive. The disciples were in a locked room, but suddenly Jesus stood with them.

'Peace be with you,' Jesus said.

At first they were afraid that he was a ghost! How could a man have entered the locked room? But when Jesus showed them the wounds where the nails had been, they believed that he was the man they had seen crucified—now alive.

Jesus told his friends that they must tell people—first in Jerusalem, then all over the world—that he had died and risen again.

Thomas had not been with the other disciples. He could not believe Jesus was alive because he had not seen him for himself. But Jesus appeared as if from nowhere again and stood among them.

'Look at my hands, Thomas. Touch the place where the sword cut my side. Stop doubting and believe!'

Thomas did not need to touch Jesus. He knew that Jesus was real and that he was alive. Thomas fell to his knees and worshipped Jesus.

'My Lord and my God,' he said.

Peter is forgiven

'Lord, you know everything. You know I love you.'

JOHN 21:17

One evening, Peter told his friends that he was going to fish in Lake Galilee. A group of them decided to go with him: Thomas, Nathanael, James, John and two of the others.

The men fished all night but by dawn, they had still caught nothing.

A man was standing on the beach watching as the boat came near to the shore and he shouted to them.

'Have you caught any fish?'

'None at all!' they replied.

'Try throwing your nets on the right side of the boat,' the man called again. 'You'll find some there.'

The fishermen had nothing to lose. They threw their nets on the other side of the boat and felt it fill with fish straight away. It was so heavy, they couldn't support the weight to bring it on to the boat.

John then realised that the man on the beach was Jesus. He told Peter. Peter grabbed his cloak

and jumped into the water so that he would be on the shore before anyone else. He wanted so much to be with Jesus. The other men rowed to shore, pulling the net of fish with them.

Jesus had a small fire ready and some bread warming.

'Bring some of your fish and come and eat with me,' Jesus said.

Peter helped bring in the catch. There were 153 large fish.

Jesus shared the bread and fish with the men and together they ate breakfast in the early morning light.

Afterwards Jesus spoke quietly to Peter.

'Peter,' he said, 'do you really love me?'

'Lord, you know I do,' said Peter.

'I want you to take care of my lambs,' Jesus replied.

But a few moments later, Jesus asked the same question again.

'Yes!' said Peter. 'You know that I love you!'

'Then take care of my sheep,' said Jesus.

But when Jesus asked again a third time, Peter was anxious. He had denied that he even knew Jesus three times. Now Jesus was asking him whether he really loved him—but he did!

'Lord, you know everything,' Peter answered. 'You know that I love you.'

'Then, Peter, I want you to feed my sheep,' said Jesus. 'Look after my followers when I have gone away; teach them, lead them and always follow me.'

The power of the Holy Spirit

'John baptised with water, but in a few days you will baptised with the Holy Spirit.'

ACTS 1:5

Jesus met his disciples many times after his resurrection from the dead. At one time he met and talked to a crowd of over 500 people.

'Stay in Jerusalem,' Jesus told them. 'I will send the Holy Spirit to you there, so you will have power to go and tell people everywhere about me. Teach them everything that I have taught you. I will always be there to help you.'

Jesus left his disciples about six weeks after he rose from the dead. They were with him on the Mount of Olives when he seemed to be covered by a cloud. Angels appeared and told them that Jesus was now with God, but that he would return again one day.

The eleven men went to Jerusalem and met the other believers. Altogether there were about 120 people.

'We need someone to replace Judas,' Peter said, 'an eyewitness to all that Jesus did and someone who saw Jesus after he rose from the dead.'

Matthias was chosen and soon they all came together to celebrate the festival of Pentecost. Suddenly, a sound like a strong wind blew through the house, and flames burned in the air, touching everyone in the room. The Holy Spirit then made it possible for them all to speak in other languages.

Jerusalem was full of people from all over the world.

'What's going on in there?' the people outside asked each other.

'There are people talking about God in my own language! But how is it possible?' said another.

Peter then came out of the house and spoke to the crowd.

'What has happened here today has fulfilled a prophecy—that God will bless his people with the Holy Spirit,' said Peter. 'Listen to me. You know that Jesus of Nazareth was here not long ago, healing people and giving sight to the blind. Despite this, you asked for him to be crucified. Well, I am here to tell you that God had planned this all along. Jesus died to prove that God has power over death.'

The people wanted to know what they could do to be saved.

'Repent and be baptised,' answered Peter. 'God will forgive you and you will receive the Holy Spirit too.'

About 3,000 people believed Peter's message that day. They saw more miracles performed and shared everything they had with each other. The Christian church was born.

Bible stories can be found as follows:

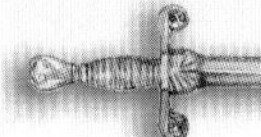

The story of creation, *Genesis 1:1—2:3*

Good and evil, *Genesis 3:1–24*

Cain and Abel, *Genesis 4:1–12, 25*

Noah's ark, *Genesis 6:1—7:4*

56, *Genesis 7:5—8:21*

The promised land, *Genesis 11:26—12:9*

The three strangers, *Genesis 18:1–14*

One good man, *Genesis 18:16—19:26*

Abraham's faith, *Genesis 22:1–18*

Ten thirsty camels, *Genesis 24:1–67*

Twin brothers, *Genesis 25:19–34; 27:1—28:5*

Jacob's ladder, *Genesis 28:10—29:14*

Abraham's descendants, *Genesis 29:15–30; 35:1–18*

Jacob's favourite son, *Genesis 37:1–35*

Dreams in Egypt, *Genesis 39:1—41:55*

God's plan for Jacob's family, *Genesis 42:1—46:7*

Moses and the Princess of Egypt, *Exodus 1:8—2:10*

The burning bush, *Exodus 2:11—4:16*

Plagues in Egypt, *Exodus 5:1–18; 7:1—12:30*

Crossing the Red Sea, *Exodus 12:31–32; 13:17—15:21*

The Ten Commandments, *Exodus 15:22—17:6; 19:10—20:17; 31:18*

Forty years in the desert, *Numbers 13:1–33; Deuteronomy 30:11–20; 31:7–8*

Rahab hides the spies, *Joshua 2:1–22*

Crossing the River Jordan, *Joshua 3:1—4:18*

The battle of Jericho, *Joshua 5:13—6:27*

Deborah, the wise judge, *Judges 4:1—5:2*

Gideon's sheepskin, *Judges 6:1–40*

The trumpet in the night, *Judges 7:1–22*

Samson, the strong man, *Judges 13:1—15:16*

Defeat of the Philistines, *Judges 16:4–30*

Ruth and Boaz, *Ruth 1:1—4:18*

Hannah keeps her promise, *1 Samuel 1:1—2:11; 3:1–21*

The first king of Israel, *1 Samuel 8:1—10:24*

Jesse's youngest son, *1 Samuel 15:1—16:13*

The giant's challenge, *1 Samuel 17:1–50*

God's gift to Solomon, *1 Kings 3:1–28*

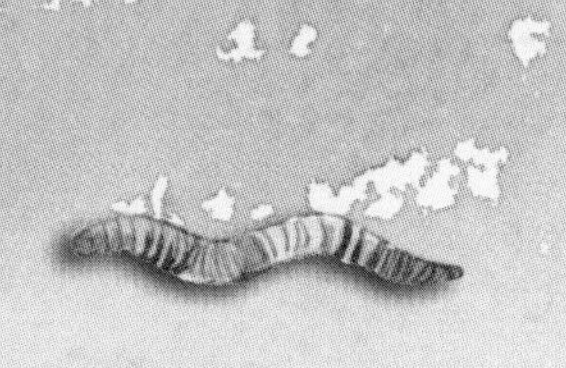

Published by the Bible Reading Fellowship
15 The Chambers, Vineyard
Abingdon, OX14 3FE
United Kingdom
Tel: +44 (0)1865 319700
Email: enquiries@brf.org.uk
Website: www.brf.org.uk

ISBN 978 1 84101 707 5

First edition 2009

Publishing Director: Annette Reynolds
Editor: Nicola Bull
Art Director: Gerald Rogers
Pre-production: Krystyna Kowalska Hewitt
Production: John Laister

Printed and bound in Singapore